the vegetarian
student cookbook

the vegetarian
student cookbook

hamlyn

An Hachette Livre UK Company
www.hachettelivre.co.uk

First published in Great Britain in 2005 by Hamlyn,
a division of Octopus Publishing Group Ltd,
2–4 Heron Quays, London E14 4JP
www.octopusbooks.co.uk

Copyright © Octopus Publishing Group Ltd 2005

ISBN: 978-0-600-61241-4

A CIP catalogue record for this book is available from
the British Library

Printed and bound in China

10 9 8 7 6 5 4 3

Notes

This books includes dishes made with nuts and nut
derivatives. It is advisable for those with known allergic
reactions to nuts and nut derivatives and those who
may be potentially vulnerable to these allergies, such
as pregnant and nursing mothers, invalids, the elderly,
babies and children, to avoid dishes made with nuts
and nut oils. It is also prudent to check the labels of
preprepared ingredients for the possible inclusion of
nut derivatives.

The Department of Health advises that eggs should not
be consumed raw. This book contains some dishes made
with raw or lightly cooked eggs. It is prudent for more
vulnerable people, such as pregnant and nursing
mothers, invalids, the elderly, babies and young
children, to avoid uncooked or lightly cooked dishes
made with eggs.

Both metric and imperial measurements are given
for the recipes. Use one set of measures only, not a
mixture of both.

The measure that has been used in the cocktail recipes
is based on a bar measure, which is 25 ml (1 fl oz).
If preferred a different volume can be used providing
the proportions are kept constant within a drink and
suitable adjustments are made to spoon measurements,
when they occur.

contents

introduction

Leaving home for the first time and moving to a new house or room in a new town or city is potentially a very daunting prospect. For many of you it will be the first time you've really had to take full responsibility for every single aspect of your life, from getting up on time in the morning, to doing all your own washing, ironing, cleaning and shopping. However, it's the all-important aspect of food that we'll be covering in the following pages. Whether you have aspirations to be a celebrity chef or you just want to make sure you don't go hungry, we'll show you how you can get by on the most basic knowledge and eat like royalty.

sorting out the basics

With more and more people choosing not to eat meat, whether for social, health or moral reasons, it's no longer seen as unusual to follow a vegetarian diet. There are obviously a number of extra considerations that need to be addressed from a dietary point of view, not least nutritional values and making sure that you eat a healthy, balanced diet, but, fear not, we'll take you through everything you need to know.

We'll also give you some advice on the foods you should be eating, the basic utensils you'll need, food preparation and kitchen hygiene. And with over 230 recipes, there's bound to be plenty to keep you cooking throughout your course. So, even if you've only ever previously ventured into the kitchen to make a late-night round of tea and toast or to put some beers in the fridge, we'll soon have you preparing a gourmet feast that will impress your new housemates.

Cooking is all about having confidence and a little imagination so that whatever is in your cupboards, you'll be able to create a meal without using baked beans or toast.

Every penny counts

As a student, you'll inevitably be living on a fairly limited budget, and while you'll want to get your priorities right in terms of the ratio between the pub fund and other expenses, it's a good idea to set aside some money for food. Investing some cash in a big food shop once a month will save you money in the long term, as it works out a lot cheaper than buying snacks and fast food or takeaways. If you're living with other people, shop together. This means you can take advantage of all those bulk-buying deals that supermarkets are so fond of, but be sensible, there's nothing worse than getting giddy with excitement at the discovery of a special offer on asparagus tips, then finding them festering at the back of the fridge a month later.

When it comes to bargain buys, however, vegetarians have the upper hand. As the clock ticks round to closing time at shops, supermarkets and fresh food markets, perishable goods can be snapped up for next to nothing. You may have to get used to hanging around the fruit and veg aisles at your local shop or loitering over the salad displays at the market, ready to pounce as the reduced stickers appear, but who cares? When the ingredients for a whole week's meals can be purchased for less than the price of a pint and a packet of peanuts, it's worth the effort.

living with carnivores

Whether you're living in hall or in a private house, the chances are that your accommodation won't be exclusively inhabited with like-minded leaf-eaters. You'll more than likely be sharing your kitchen and cooking facilities with firmly committed carnivores. So, if the sight of raw meat makes you feel squeamish, or if you have to leave the house for a breath of fresh air whenever meat is being cooked, then you may need to start by trying to overcome some of your phobias.

Basically, when it comes to living together, it's all about give and take: a little consideration on the part of your meat-eating friends will obviously be required, but ultimately it will be down to you to remind them (politely) not to use your chopping boards, knives and pans nor to leave uncovered raw meat in the fridge. Here are a few suggestions to help organize your kitchen storage arrangements that may help to prevent any misunderstandings: have your own cupboard for pots and pans, label your cooking knives or keep them in a separate drawer and designate a meat-free shelf in the fridge. You should try to set out a few ground rules like these from the beginning, and, although you don't want to create a first impression of being bossy and

a bit sad, it's better to start as you mean to continue, rather than ending up by falling out with your friends later on in the year.

Although phrases like, 'It's almost vegetarian, it's just got a bit of ham in it', or 'I used your pan, but I only cooked fish, so it should be fine', may send shivers down your spine, try to have a bit of patience; the concept of vegetarianism can sometimes be difficult for the uninitiated to grasp. Vegetarian food has come along way since the delights of a lentil loaf and lettuce, with ingredients and flavours inspired by international cuisine. Persevere, and you never know, you may even end up by introducing your housemates to a whole new culinary experience and, although you probably won't be rewarded with complete converts to a meat-free diet, with the skills and recipes that you learn here, you will certainly open their eyes (and stomachs) to the endless possibilities that vegetarian food can offer.

the bare essentials

If you're moving into a hall of residence or a shared house, you may well be starting from scratch in terms of utensils and equipment, bar the odd can opener or tea-stained mug left behind by a previous occupant. It's best to start with a clean slate, and as long as you have a cooker in working order you're in business. If you can find out who you'll be living with before you move in, it might be a good idea to divide the equipment list so that everyone buys a couple of utensils. There are countless gadgets on the market, but many of them will remain unused, gathering dust and cluttering your kitchen, so it's best to stick to things that you're actually going to use. Let's face it: you should be able to make it through the year without any culinary mishaps resulting from the lack of a lemon zester or a set of star-shaped pastry cutters. So, here's a list of the equipment and utensils that you shouldn't leave home without:

Set of saucepans
These really are essential if you're planning to do any cooking at all. Buy three if possible – small, medium and large – as this will enable you to cook different ingredients at the same time. A large frying pan with a lid is also great for one-pot meals and means you won't necessarily have to invest in a casserole dish as well.

Set of knives
Again, very important. Try and buy two or three different types, as you'll need one for slicing bread, another for large vegetables and a smaller paring knife for onions, garlic and other smaller vegetables. Make sure they're all kept sharp.

Chopping boards
It's a good idea to have at least two chopping boards (use one for strongly-flavoured vegetables, such as onions, which may taint fruit). Plastic ones are the most practical and take far less time to wash and dry than wooden ones. Bacteria can gather in the cracks of old wooden boards, so replace them regularly.

Wok

Not essential but extremely useful. Stir-fries are cheap, quick and easy to prepare, and a real vegetarian staple.

Utensils

You can buy these in sets – make sure the set includes a wooden spoon, spatula, ladle and potato masher. You'll also need a can opener, vegetable/potato peeler and a grater (and probably a bottle opener, as well).

Mixing bowl

Great for whisking eggs and making sauces.

Ovenproof dish

Very handy if you want to make veggie lasagnes, stews or casseroles.

Colander

A versatile piece of equipment. Not only will it ensure that your rice and pasta aren't waterlogged when you serve them, but a metal one can also double as a vegetable steamer.

Store cupboard essentials

There are some ingredients that you should always have to hand, so that by buying just a couple of extras you can rustle up a quick meal. Many of these are basic ingredients that you'll see crop up again and again in many of the recipes in this book.

☐ **Salt and pepper** (freshly ground black pepper is best)
☐ **Good quality olive oil** (for dressings, marinades and grilling vegetables or veggie burgers and sausages)
☐ **Vegetable oil**
☐ **Butter or margarine**
☐ **Eggs**
☐ **Milk**
☐ **Onions**
☐ **Garlic**
☐ **Rice** (brown is better for you, but it takes longer to cook)
☐ **Pasta**
☐ **Potatoes**
☐ **Flour**
☐ **Dried spices** (curry powder, ground coriander, ground cumin, paprika and turmeric are used a lot)
☐ **Dried mixed herbs**
☐ **Mustard**
☐ **Cans of chopped tomatoes**
☐ **Tomato purée**
☐ **Quorn** (available as mince, steaks, sausages and burgers)
☐ **Soya** (available in different forms)

preparation

To get a good grip on the whole cooking experience, there are a couple of things to consider before you even think about letting yourself loose in the kitchen or trying to follow a recipe. As with learning a language, the more you practise the better you'll become and the more confidence you'll have to try adding your own personal twist to the recipes.

Before you begin

First of all, make sure you have all the ingredients you need. This may sound obvious, but there's nothing worse than being halfway through a recipe and suddenly realizing that someone has helped themselves to the vital ingredient.

It's a good idea to do all the peeling, measuring, chopping, etc. before you start. Put each ingredient into a bowl or on a plate, then you can cook without interruption.

If you're using the oven, make sure you preheat it to the correct temperature before you put the food in.

Rinsing

Rinse rice thoroughly before cooking to get rid of the starch. This will stop the rice sticking together when it is cooked. When cooking potatoes, drop them into a pan of cold water as you're chopping them, then rinse the potatoes and change the water before cooking.

Cooking

Always make sure the water is boiling before adding rice or pasta.

Try not to open the oven door too often when cooking – this lowers the temperature and will affect the cooking time.

Don't stir spaghetti and tagliatelle while they're cooking, as this will make them knotty when you come to serve them.

Preparing vegetables

Scrub vegetables rather than peeling them, if you can, because many of the nutrients are found in the skins.

Try to cut vegetables into nice, large pieces, as this keeps more of the nutrients intact.

It's amazing how many injuries one can sustain from preparing vegetables. Knives are obviously far more efficient if they're kept really sharp, but you should be careful when chopping. When you are preparing round vegetables, such as courgettes or carrots, slice them in half lengthways first so that you've got a flat surface. For pure aesthetics, try slicing vegetables on the diagonal; this is great for stir-fries or char-grilled veggies, as they will cook quickly but still retain their bite.

Cabbage

Peel and discard the tough, outer leaves. Rinse the heart under cold running water then cut it into large pieces, otherwise the cabbage will become waterlogged and much of the goodness will be lost. Cabbage is better steamed than boiled.

Carrots

Peel, using a vegetable peeler, or scrub baby carrots. Trim the ends, then cut in half lengthways and slice into semicircles or baton shapes.

Chillies

Cut the chilli in half lengthways then scrape out the seeds, using the tip of a sharp knife. The seeds and oil are extremely hot, so you should either protect your hands (gloves or sandwich bags will do the trick) or make sure you wash your hands thoroughly after handling chillies.

Garlic

To peel garlic, place the clove under the flat of a large knife and press down firmly with your fist. This makes it easy to remove the skin and finely slice the clove.

Green beans

Rinse well, then top and tail. Leave beans whole or slice in half and steam or cook in boiling water.

Onions

Before chopping an onion, peel it, then rinse it under cold, running water. This should help to stop your eyes watering.

If a recipe requires lots of chopped or grated onion (or cheese, carrot, fresh breadcrumbs, etc.), you can use a food processor, if you have one. For finely chopped garlic, onion or ginger, use the smallest setting on a grater.

Potatoes

For baked or roast potatoes – scrub under running water and leave unpeeled.

For chips – peel, slice in half then slice into baton shapes. Leave to soak in a pan of water until you are ready to cook.

For mash – peel and cut each one into small dice, so that it cooks quickly and is easy to mash.

For potato salad – use small, whole new potatoes. Scrub them well and boil until cooked through, then rinse well under cold, running water.

For gratin – peel and slice thinly into rounds, rinse well and pat dry.

read the label

Just because a food product doesn't contain meat or any obviously animal-derived ingredients, it doesn't mean that it's necessarily suitable for vegetarians. Naturally, the extent to which you read your food labels depends on how strict a vegetarian you are, but it is always wise to know exactly what you're eating. You may be surprised to learn that many seemingly innocuous foods contain animal-derived products. Here is just a small selection:

Biscuits
Many varieties contain animal fats, so always check the label.

Cheese
This is generally made with animal rennet. However, there are plenty of vegetarian cheeses available, from Cheddar to Parmesan, so you shouldn't have any problems satisfying those cheese cravings.

Chocolate
This is often made with whey and emulsifiers. Vegetarian brands are available from health food stores.

Crisps
Many varieties use whey as a flavour-carrier and the only true vegetarian flavour is ready-salted.

Ice cream
This often includes dairy fats, but check for non-dairy fats and eggs.

Jelly
Most brands contain gelatine.

Margarine and butter
Some brands contain animal fat and/or gelatine; however, pure butter is suitable for vegetarians.

Soup
Even a purely vegetable-based soup may use a meat stock, so always check the label.

Sweets
Many, particularly hard or boiled sweets, contain gelatine.

Wine
Many wines contain animal products. There are vegetarian wines, but you may have to search around to find them.

Worcestershire sauce
This pungent sauce, made to a secret recipe, includes anchovies.

Toothpaste
Many brands contain glycerine, so be careful when choosing your toothpaste.

Kitchen hygiene

As part of your choice to follow a vegetarian diet, you may feel strongly about any contact with meat or meat products, but remember that it's not just meat-eaters who are susceptible to food poisoning or food-related illnesses: it's just as important for you to follow a few simple rules when preparing and cooking your food.

✻Always wash your hands thoroughly in hot, soapy water before you start cooking.

✻If you're sharing your fridge with meat-eaters, make sure they keep any meat or fish on the bottom shelf, so that the juices don't drip on to and contaminate other food.

✻Wash salad, fruit and vegetables thoroughly before preparing them – you don't know how many people handled them before they went into your shopping basket.

✻If you're reheating food, do this only once and make sure the food is piping hot all the way through.

✻Use really hot water when washing-up – the hotter the water, the better it will be at killing germs.

balancing act

If you're following a vegetarian diet, you will need to think more about food than your meat-eating counterparts. Although it is relatively easy to get all the vitamins and minerals that your body requires without eating meat or fish, it is important to be aware of the types of foods that supply high levels of protein and minerals. While it's often cheap and easy to live off pasta, snacks and fast foods when you're a student, it's also extremely important to look after your health, particularly around exam time, when you will be working long hours and putting your body and brain under extra pressure. Add to the equation the odd late night and over-indulgence in alcohol that are synonymous with student life and you've got every reason you could possibly need to make sure you eat a healthy, balanced diet. Let's take a look at some of the key areas that you should be thinking about in terms of your diet and at the foods that will provide the minerals and vitamins you need.

Carbohydrates

This is an easy one for vegetarians. Good carbohydrates should make up the biggest proportion of your meals, as this is where you get 'energy'. Carbohydrate-rich foods include bread, rice, pasta and some vegetables, such as potatoes.

Protein

This is where you need to start making an effort. Be aware of what you're eating and make sure that you include sufficient protein in your diet. Good sources of protein include dairy products, grains and cereals, pulses, seeds and eggs.

Iron

Leafy green vegetables are where it's at in terms of iron intake. Pulses, eggs and lentils are other good sources.

Calcium

We're told as soon as we can walk that we need calcium for our teeth and bones, but although dairy products are the major provider, you can also get calcium from leafy green vegetables, seeds and dried fruit.

Vitamins

You should be able to obtain all the vitamins you require if you eat a balanced diet that's rich in fresh fruit and vegetables. Tomatoes, carrots and leafy green vegetables are particularly good for vitamin A; eat nuts, seeds and cereals for your B vitamins; most fruits, salads and leafy green vegetables will provide you with vitamin C; vitamin E is found in eggs and cereals, and, for vitamin D, you'll need to get outside. The body produces its own when the skin is exposed to sunlight, so don't lie in bed all day when you've got a hangover.

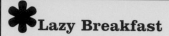

menu planners

✳ Lazy Breakfast

If you remember your mother telling you that breakfast is the most important meal of the day, now's the time to put that advice into practice. Even if you're not too strict about the cut-off point between breakfast and lunch, you should always line your stomach before embarking on any activity. These recipes will alleviate any guilt you might have about lying in bed all morning, and should help you get rid of that hangover, too!

Eggs Benedict page 25

Herb Omelette with Mustard Mushrooms page 27

Spanish Omelette page 28

Baked Eggs page 88

Stir-fried Mixed Mushrooms page 144

Fresh Fruit Salad page 196

Cranberry Flapjacks page 228

✸ Lunch on the Move

While a quick sandwich on the run may be the usual state of affairs when it comes to student lunches, just think how much nicer a home-made snack will taste. You'll certainly save some money by making your own lunch and, if you live close enough to your college, it's even worth popping home. We've got everything from sandwiches to soups here, so there's no excuse to make do with a soggy egg roll from the canteen. Many of these recipes can be cooked in advance, or made in bulk, so you've got lunch for a week.

✸ Converting the Carnivores

This selection of meals will satisfy even the most committed meat-eaters, and the recipes are ideal if you're cooking for a mixture of veggies and non-veggies.

✸ Brain Food

Here are some recipes that will keep you feeling alert for all those late-night exam revision sessions.

brilliant breakfasts

4 **eggs**

2 slices **bread**

25 g (1 oz) **butter**

salt and **pepper**

PREP

5

COOK

5

SERVES

2

fast

easy

tasty

boiled eggs with toast

Eggs are very quick and simple to cook and can be eaten at any time of the day – for breakfast, lunch or dinner or as a post-pub snack. They are the ideal fast food.

1 Boil a saucepan of water then carefully add the eggs to the pan using a spoon so they do not crack. Boil for 4–5 minutes – the whites should be set but the yolks still runny (boil for an extra couple of minutes if you want the yolks to be set as well).

2 Meanwhile, toast then butter the bread.

3 Remove the eggs from the pan with the spoon and crack open. Sprinkle with salt and pepper and eat with the toast.

fried eggs

1 tablespoon
vegetable oil

2 **eggs**

For a quick snack simply eat with toast or for the full breakfast serve with grilled tomatoes and mushrooms and fried bread. If you want your yolks better cooked, flip the eggs over just before you take them out of the pan.

COOK

2

1 Heat the oil in a frying pan until it is really hot but not smoking or burning.

2 Break an egg into a cup, remove any eggshell, then tip the egg into the frying pan. The white should begin to set immediately. Repeat with the other egg.

3 Turn the heat down to medium and spoon the oil over the eggs so the tops cook as well. Cook for about a minute until the whites are set but the yolks are still runny. Use a fish slice or spatula to remove the eggs from the pan so that the yolks don't break.

SERVES

1

snack

fun

fast

poached eggs

1 tablespoon **vinegar**

2 **eggs**

COOK

5

Although poaching eggs may seem to be a bit fiddly, if you use very fresh eggs you shouldn't have any problems. Eat with baked beans on toast for a healthy and tasty start to the day.

SERVES

1

cheap

best

yum!

1 Pour about 4 cm (1½ inches) of water into a saucepan or frying pan and add the vinegar (this helps the white to stick to the yolk). Bring the water to the boil, then turn down the heat so it is just simmering (not boiling violently).

2 Break an egg into a cup and slide it carefully into the water. If you need to, gently stir the water around the egg so that the white makes a neat round shape. Repeat with the other egg.

3 Poach for 3–5 minutes over a very low heat, until the whites are set but the yolks are still runny. Take the poached eggs out of the pan with a spoon and eat straight away with buttered toast.

scrambled eggs

2 **eggs**

1 tablespoon **milk**

15 g (½ oz) **butter**

salt and **pepper**

If you want to jazz up simple scrambled eggs, try adding fresh chopped herbs or grated cheese, and serve with croissants or ciabatta. A real treat.

1 Crack the eggs into a bowl and beat with a fork, adding the milk and a sprinkling of salt and pepper.

2 Melt the butter in a saucepan (ideally use a nonstick saucepan because scrambled egg tends to stick) over a low heat, then add the egg mixture. Stir the eggs with a wooden spoon until the eggs have scrambled and have just set, then take off the heat and eat straight away with toast.

tasty

feast

sexy

40 g (1½ oz) **butter**

1 kg (2 lb) fresh **spinach**, washed

2 large **tomatoes**, skinned and finely chopped

grated **nutmeg**

6 large **eggs**

150 ml (¼ pint) **crème fraîche**

50 ml (2 fl oz) **double cream**

40 g (1½ oz) **Cheddar cheese**, grated

40 g (1½ oz) **Parmesan cheese**, grated

salt and **pepper**

PREP

15

COOK

20

SERVES

6

star

share

yum!

eggs florentine

A special kind of brunch – just grab some mates and the Sunday newspapers and chill out after eating this filling and delicious dish.

1 Heat the oven to 220°C (425°F), Gas Mark 7.

2 Melt half the butter in a large saucepan and add the spinach with the water that clings to the leaves. Cover the pan and cook over a low heat until soft. Drain well, add the tomatoes, a dash of grated nutmeg and salt and pepper.

3 Use the rest of the butter to grease 6 small 175 ml (6 fl oz) dishes. Divide the spinach equally among the dishes, making a hole in the centre of each one for an egg, and leaving a 1 cm (½ inch) space between the spinach and the top of the dish.

4 Break an egg into the centre of each dish and sprinkle with salt and pepper.

5 Mix together the crème fraîche and cream. Spoon over the eggs and sprinkle with the Cheddar and Parmesan.

6 Put the dishes on a baking sheet and bake in the oven for 12 minutes, until the egg whites are set but the yolks are still runny.

7 Take the dishes out of the oven and put under a hot grill until the cheese is bubbling. Dish up straight away.

eggs benedict

This classic breakfast dish is renowned as a hangover cure. It might be worth trying if you are suffering from the night before ...

8 large **field mushrooms**

2 tablespoons **olive oil**

8 **eggs**

1 tablespoon **vinegar**

4 **muffins**

25 g (1 oz) **butter**

Hollandaise sauce:

3 **egg yolks**

1 tablespoon **water**

125 g (4 oz) **butter**, softened

large pinch of **salt**

2 pinches of **cayenne pepper**

1 teaspoon **lemon juice**

1 tablespoon **single cream**

1 Heat the oven to 200°C (400°F), Gas Mark 6.

2 Put the mushrooms, with the caps facing down, in a large ovenproof dish. Drizzle over the olive oil, cover with foil and cook in the oven for 20 minutes.

3 To make the sauce, beat together the egg yolks and water in a bowl over a saucepan of simmering water, until the mixture is pale. Gradually add the butter, a few small pieces at a time, and beat until the sauce thickens. Add the salt, 1 pinch of cayenne pepper and the lemon juice. Stir in the cream then remove from the heat and keep warm.

4 Poach the eggs until just set (see page 22).

5 Meanwhile, cut the muffins in half, toast them and spread with butter. Put a mushroom, cap side down, on each muffin half and top with a poached egg. Dollop a little sauce over each egg, sprinkle with the rest of the cayenne pepper and eat straight away.

posh

fancy

feast

omelette with cherry tomatoes

3 tablespoons **olive oil**

125 g (4 oz) **cherry tomatoes**

2 tablespoons chopped mixed **herbs** (such as basil, chives, mint, tarragon or thyme)

1 teaspoon grated **lemon rind**

3 **eggs**

1 tablespoon **red pesto**

2 tablespoons **milk**

salt and **pepper**

PREP

5

COOK

8

SERVES

1

crisp

fast

fresh

This fresh-tasting omelette is perfect for a late breakfast or even as a summer lunch with a green salad and a decadently cold glass of white wine.

1 Heat 2 tablespoons of the oil in a frying pan and fry the tomatoes, herbs and lemon rind for 3 minutes until the tomatoes start to soften. Take off the heat and keep warm.

2 Crack the eggs into a bowl and beat well. Add the pesto, milk and a dash of salt and pepper and beat again.

3 Melt the rest of the oil in a frying pan over a medium heat, then tip in the eggs.

4 Leave for a few seconds then, using a fork or spoon, scrape the mixture away from the edge of the pan into the centre, so the egg mixture runs to the sides. Do this a couple of times until the egg mixture is set, which should take 3–4 minutes.

5 Spoon on the tomato mixture, flip over the omelette, cook for another minute then eat straight away.

herb omelette with mustard mushrooms

This dish is so easy to make that you can knock it up in just quarter of an hour. The mustard gives the mushrooms a bit of a kick, and you can put whatever herbs you like into the omelette.

PREP

5

COOK

10

SERVES

2

50 g (2 oz) **butter**, softened

1 tablespoon **wholegrain mustard**

4 flat **mushrooms**

4 **eggs**

2 tablespoons chopped mixed **herbs** (such as chives, parsley or tarragon)

salt and **pepper**

1 In a bowl mix 40 g (1½ oz) of the butter with the mustard, then spread over the undersides of the mushrooms. Place the mushrooms, with the undersides facing up, under a hot grill for 5–6 minutes until golden. Remove and keep warm.

2 Meanwhile, crack the eggs into a bowl and beat well. Add the herbs and a dash of salt and pepper and beat again.

3 Melt the rest of the butter in a frying pan over a medium heat. When the butter starts to foam, but before it goes brown, tip in the eggs.

4 Leave the eggs for a few seconds then, using a fork or spoon, scrape the mixture away from the edge of the pan into the centre, so the egg mixture runs to the sides. Do this a couple of times until the egg is set. Cook for another 30 seconds until the bottom is golden but the top is slightly runny and creamy.

5 Flip the omelette over in half, slide on to a plate and cut in half. Divide between two plates and dish up with the mushrooms and some crusty bread.

tangy

juicy

mates

150 ml (¼ pint) **olive oil**

4 large **potatoes**, thinly sliced

1 large **onion**, thinly sliced

4–5 large **eggs**

salt and **pepper**

PREP

10

COOK

50

SERVES

4

snack

fun

tasty

spanish omelette

This filling omelette, known as a tortilla in Spain, can be served hot, warm or cold. It's a great snack for whenever you feel a bit peckish, and you can make your own variations by adding mushrooms, peppers, sweetcorn or whatever you have handy in your fridge.

1 Heat the oil in a large frying pan. Add the potatoes and onion, cover and cook over a low heat, until the potatoes are tender but not coloured. This will take about 30 minutes.

2 Lift the vegetables out of the pan and drain them in a colander. Keep the oil from the pan.

3 In a bowl beat the eggs and season with salt and pepper. Add the vegetables, pressing them down well, then leave for about 15 minutes.

4 In a clean pan, heat 2–3 tablespoons of the reserved oil. Add the egg mixture and quickly spread it out with a knife. Turn down the heat and cook gently, shaking the pan occasionally to prevent the mixture from sticking. When it starts to brown underneath and to shrink from the edge of the pan, which should take about 15 minutes, take the pan off the heat.

5 Flip the omelette over and cook the other side for another 3–5 minutes, or until the tortilla is cooked and brown on both sides.

mustard rarebit

PREP

5

COOK

10

SERVES

4

You can tart up this rarebit as much as you like. Why not try using blue cheese, such as Stilton, or add a thick layer of chutney under the cheese? You could also add walnuts, olives or capers to the cheese mix – just experiment!

25 g (1 oz) **butter**

4 **spring onions**, thinly sliced

250 g (8 oz) **Cheddar** or **Red Leicester cheese**, grated

50 ml (2 fl oz) **beer**

2 teaspoons **mustard**

4 slices **white bread**

pepper

1 Melt the butter in a frying pan, then add the spring onions and fry for 5 minutes, until the onions have softened.

2 Turn down the heat and stir in the cheese, beer and mustard. Add a good dash of pepper then melt the cheese mixture slowly.

3 Meanwhile, toast the bread lightly on both sides and place on a grill pan. Pour the cheese mixture over the toast and grill under a hot grill for 1 minute, until bubbling and golden.

tangy

mates

telly

1 tablespoon **vegetable oil**

1 small **red onion**, finely chopped

2 **celery sticks**, finely chopped

1 **garlic clove**, crushed

200 g (7 oz) can chopped **tomatoes**

150 ml (¼ pint) **vegetable stock**

1 tablespoon **soy sauce**

1 tablespoon **dark brown sugar**

2 teaspoons **mustard**

400 g (13 oz) can **mixed beans**, drained and rinsed

2 slices **white bread**

2 tablespoons chopped **parsley**

PREP

COOK

SERVES

great

boston baked beans

Homemade baked beans are a revelation. When you've tried them once, you'll realize it's definitely worth taking the time to cook your own rather than opening a can of ready-made beans.

1 Heat the oil in a large saucepan, add the onion and fry over a low heat for 5 minutes, or until softened. Add the celery and garlic and fry for another 1–2 minutes.

2 Add the tomatoes, stock and soy sauce, then turn up the heat until it boils. Turn down the heat so it is just simmering and cook for about 15 minutes, or until the sauce begins to thicken.

3 Add the sugar, mustard and beans and cook for another 5 minutes, or until the beans are heated through. Meanwhile, toast the bread lightly on both sides. Stir in the parsley then dollop on to the toast and tuck in.

mushrooms on toast

This is a very simple but irresistible dish. It's not for calorie-counters, although you can substitute low-fat crème fraîche for the double cream and have toast instead of fried bread if you prefer.

1 Sprinkle the mushrooms with the lemon juice and leave for 5 minutes.

2 Melt the butter in a saucepan. Add the mushrooms and cook over a medium heat for 2 minutes. Add the herbs, cream and a dash of salt and pepper. Turn down the heat and simmer gently for about 7 minutes, or until the mushrooms are cooked through.

3 Meanwhile, heat the oil in a frying pan. Add the bread and fry until golden brown on both sides, then drain on kitchen paper. Divide the mushrooms equally among the slices of bread and top with the cheese. Place under a hot grill and cook until the cheese is bubbling. Serve immediately.

PREP

10

COOK

15

SERVES

4

hot

fab!

snack

425 g (14 oz) **button mushrooms**, sliced

1 tablespoon **lemon juice**

1 tablespoon **butter**

½ tablespoon chopped **basil**

2 tablespoons chopped **parsley**

2 tablespoons **double cream**

2 tablespoons **vegetable oil**

4 slices **bread**

50 g (2 oz) **Cheddar cheese**, sliced

salt and **pepper**

1 **orange**

225 g (7½ oz) **plain flour**

2 teaspoons **baking powder**

50 g (2 oz) **oatmeal**, plus extra for sprinkling

75 g (3 oz) **soft brown sugar**

200 g (7 oz) **Greek yogurt**

4 tablespoons **vegetable oil**

150 ml (¼ pint) **milk**

1 **egg**

200 g (7 oz) **milk chocolate**, chopped

PREP

COOK

20

MAKES

10

tasty

share

mates

chocolate and orange muffins

If you want to make smaller muffins use ordinary paper cake cases and reduce the cooking time by 5 minutes.

1 Heat the oven to 200°C (400°F), Gas Mark 6.

2 Grate the rind from the orange. In a large bowl mix the flour and baking powder. Stir in the orange rind, oatmeal and sugar.

3 In another bowl beat the yogurt with the oil, milk and egg and add to the flour mixture along with the chocolate. Using a metal spoon, carefully blend the ingredients together until they have just combined, adding a little more milk if the mixture is too dry.

4 Divide the mixture among 10 paper muffin cases or similar and sprinkle the top with extra oatmeal. Bake in the oven for 15–20 minutes until the muffins have risen and are firm.

blueberry and vanilla muffins

PREP

5

COOK

15

MAKES

10

These classic American muffins are packed with the goodness of blueberries, just watch out though – they taste so good that they won't last long.

150 g (5 oz) **ground almonds**

150 g (5 oz) **caster sugar**

50 g (2 oz) **self-raising flour**

175 g (6 oz) **butter**, melted

4 **egg whites**

1 teaspoon **vanilla essence**

150 g (5 oz) **blueberries**

1 Heat the oven to 220°C (425°F), Gas Mark 7.

2 In a large bowl mix together the almonds, sugar, flour and butter. Add the egg whites and vanilla and mix until you make a smooth paste.

3 Divide the mixture among 10 paper muffin cases or similar and scatter with the blueberries.

4 Bake in the oven for 15 minutes until just firm in the centre.

fruity

keeps

pals

125 g (4 oz) **plain flour**

3 tablespoons **soft brown sugar**

2 teaspoons **baking powder**

1 **egg**, beaten

50 ml (2 fl oz) **milk**

50 ml (2 fl oz) **vegetable oil**

2 large ripe **bananas**, roughly mashed

Topping:

1 tablespoon **linseeds**

25 g (1 oz) **self-raising flour**

15 g (½ oz) **butter**, softened and cut into cubes

40 g (1½ oz) **demerara sugar**

½ teaspoon ground **cinnamon**

1 tablespoon **water**

PREP

COOK

35

MAKES

6

fresh

moist

fast

banana muffins with cinnamon

These tasty muffins make a delicious breakfast treat as well as a great snack for when you are rushing about and need a boost of energy.

1 Heat the oven to 200°C (400°F), Gas Mark 6.

2 Start by making the topping. Put the linseeds in a blender or food processor and blend for 30 seconds.

3 Put the self-raising flour in a bowl and mix in the butter until the mixture looks like fine breadcrumbs. Add the sugar, linseeds and cinnamon, then stir in the water and mix well.

4 To make the muffins, mix the plain flour, sugar and baking powder in a large bowl, then make a hole in the centre.

5 In another bowl, mix the egg, milk and oil together, then pour into the flour mixture. Stir until it is just mixed together, then stir in the bananas but don't mix too much.

6 Divide the mixture among 6 paper muffin cases or similar, then sprinkle a little of the topping over each muffin. Bake in the oven for 20–35 minutes until firm.

granola

This is delicious eaten on its own, or you could have it with milk, yogurt or fresh fruit for a healthy breakfast that will set you up for the rest of the day.

1 Heat the oven to 160°C (325°F), Gas Mark 3.

2 Put the butter, honey and vanilla essence in a saucepan and cook over a medium heat, stirring occasionally, for 5 minutes or until the honey and butter are combined.

3 Put the rest of the ingredients, except the fruit, in a large bowl and mix well. Carefully stir in the butter mixture.

4 Spread the mixture over the base of a large, nonstick tin and bake in the oven for 20 minutes or until the grains are crisp and browned. Stir occasionally so it doesn't stick.

5 Take out of the oven and leave to cool, then stir in the dried fruit.

PREP

10

COOK

5

SERVES

10

crisp

snack

keeps

75 g (3 oz) **butter**

5 tablespoons **honey**

1 teaspoon **vanilla essence**

300 g (10 oz) **rolled oats**

50 g (2 oz) dried shredded **coconut**

50 g (2 oz) flaked **almonds**

3 tablespoons **sunflower seeds**

3 tablespoons **pumpkin seeds**

1 tablespoon **sesame seeds**

1 tablespoon **linseeds**

75 g (3 oz) **rye flakes**

75 g (3 oz) ready-to-eat mixed **dried fruit salad**, roughly chopped

75 g (3 oz) **rolled oats**

100 ml (3½ fl oz) **milk**

75 ml (3 fl oz) **water**

1 tablespoon **brown sugar**

1 large ripe **banana**, finely sliced

2 tablespoons **pumpkin seeds**

PREP

COOK

SERVES

2

banana porridge

If you don't like bananas, why not try adding a handful of fresh berries or a few roughly chopped dried apricots instead? Just use whatever fruit you have handy to make a hearty breakfast.

1 Put the oats, milk, water, sugar and banana in a large saucepan and bring to the boil, stirring all the time. Turn down the heat and simmer, stirring occasionally, for about 5–10 minutes or until it reaches a consistency you like.

2 Spoon into bowls, pour over a little more milk then scatter over the pumpkin seeds and eat straight away.

blackberry and apple muesli

This is great brain food, and will release energy slowly throughout the day so you can focus on studying ... or simply having fun.

1 Mix together the oats, bran, sunflower seeds, nuts and sultanas.

2 Toss the sliced apple in the lemon juice so it doesn't go brown.

3 Spoon the muesli mixture into 4 bowls and top with the apple slices and blackberries. Enjoy with milk or yogurt.

PREP

10

COOK

0

SERVES

4

fruity

star

fab!

10 tablespoons **rolled oats**

1 tablespoon **bran**

1 tablespoon **sunflower seeds**

4 tablespoons chopped mixed **nuts**

4 tablespoons **sultanas**

2 **apples**, peeled, cored and thinly sliced

1 tablespoon **lemon juice**

250 g (8 oz) **blackberries**

sticky apricot muesli bars

125 g (4 oz) **butter**

125 g (4 oz) **soft brown sugar**

4 tablespoons **golden syrup**

125 g (4 oz) ready-to-eat **dried apricots**, roughly chopped

125 g (4 oz) **rolled oats**

25 g (1 oz) **linseeds**

25 g (1 oz) **sunflower seeds**

25 g (1 oz) **sesame seeds**

25 g (1 oz) **pumpkin seeds**

50 g (2 oz) **self-raising flour**

PREP

10

COOK

30

MAKES

10

easy

gooey

share

These tasty, chewy flapjack-style bars are made with a mixture of fruit, seeds and oats. They can be kept in an airtight container for up to 5 days ... if they last that long.

1 Heat the oven to 180°C (350°F), Gas Mark 4.

2 Line the base and sides of a 20 cm (8 inch) shallow square tin with greaseproof paper.

3 Melt the butter, sugar and syrup in a large saucepan over a medium heat. Stir in the apricots, oats, seeds and flour and mix well. Spoon the mixture into the tin and press flat, then bake in the oven for 20–25 minutes or until brown.

4 Leave to cool for 10 minutes, then cut into 10 bars and allow to cool completely and crisp up before you eat them.

banana and three-seed energy bars

These homemade energy bars will give you a fantastic boost of long-term energy, so enjoy them for breakfast or have one before a big night out.

1 Heat the oven to 180°C (350°F), Gas Mark 4.

2 Line the base and sides of an 18 cm (7 inch) square baking tin or similar with greaseproof paper.

3 Melt the butter and syrup in a large saucepan until dissolved. Remove from the heat, add the rest of the ingredients and mix well.

4 Pour the mixture into the tin, level the surface and bake in the oven for 20–30 minutes or until golden brown (the mixture will still be very soft in the centre).

5 Leave to cool in the tin for 10 minutes, then cut into 9 squares. Leave to crisp up and cool completely then eat or store in an airtight container.

PREP

10

COOK

30

MAKES

9

party

keeps

crisp

100 g (3½ oz) **butter**

3 tablespoons **golden syrup**

150 g (5 oz) **rolled oats**

2 large ripe **bananas**, sliced

100 g (3½ oz) ready-to-eat **dried prunes**, roughly chopped

25 g (1 oz) **pumpkin seeds**

25 g (1 oz) **sunflower seeds**

25 g (1 oz) **sesame seeds**

soups and salads

300 g (10 oz) can condensed **tomato soup**

400 g (13 oz) can **tomatoes**, sieved

325 g (11 oz) can **sweetcorn**, drained

1 tablespoon **soy sauce**

3–6 drops **Tabasco sauce**

1 teaspoon chopped **oregano**

½ teaspoon **sugar**

125 g (4 oz) **Cheddar cheese**, grated

PREP

5

COOK

10

SERVES

4

fab!

tangy

hot

easy tomato soup

This classic soup can be made more or less spicy depending on how much Tabasco sauce you add. Perfect for a cold winter's day.

1 Put all the ingredients, except the cheese, in a large saucepan and cook over a medium heat stirring all the time. Bring to the boil, then turn down the heat and simmer, uncovered, for 3 minutes.

2 Pour the soup into ovenproof bowls, sprinkle with cheese and place under a hot grill for 3–5 minutes until the cheese is bubbling. Delicious with crusty wholemeal bread.

oven-baked vegetable soup

This is the heartiest of winter soups – a meal in itself. It's not only extremely easy to make but is very cheap too.

tasty

green

telly

1 Heat the oven to 200°C (400°F), Gas Mark 6.

2 Toss the vegetables with the oil and honey in a large bowl then tip into a roasting tin. Add the herbs and pop in the oven. Roast for 25–30 minutes until the vegetables are golden and tender. Add the tomatoes, turn down the oven to 190°C (375°F), Gas Mark 5 and roast for another 25–30 minutes.

3 Remove the herbs, put the vegetables in a blender or food processor and blend until smooth with as much stock as you need.

4 Pour the soup into a large ovenproof dish, add some salt and pepper and bake for 20 minutes. Perfect with buttered toast.

1 **onion**, roughly chopped

2 **garlic cloves**, chopped

2 large **carrots**, thinly sliced

1 **leek**, trimmed and thickly sliced

1 large **parsnip**, cut into cubes

175 g (6 oz) **swede**, cut into cubes

4 tablespoons **vegetable oil**

2 teaspoons **honey**

4 **rosemary** sprigs

2 **bay leaves**

4 ripe **tomatoes**, quartered

1.2 litres (2 pints) **vegetable stock**

salt and **pepper**

2 tablespoons **vegetable oil**

1 large **onion**, chopped

1–2 **garlic cloves**, crushed

1 tablespoon finely grated fresh **root ginger**

375 g (12 oz) **carrots**, sliced

900 ml (1½ pints) **vegetable stock**

2 tablespoons **lemon juice**

salt and **pepper**

4 teaspoons **soured cream**, to serve

20

COOK

30

SERVES

4

great

fun

juicy

carrot and ginger soup

Carrot and ginger make a great combination, and because ginger is known to help cure stomach complaints it's perfect if you have over-indulged the night before.

1 Heat the oil in a saucepan over a low heat, add the onion, garlic and ginger and cook for 5–6 minutes until soft.

2 Add the carrots and stock and bring to the boil, then turn down the heat and simmer for about 15–20 minutes or until the carrots are tender.

3 Pour the soup into a blender or food processor and blend with the lemon juice until smooth. Sieve the soup then pour it back into the saucepan and reheat it. Add a good dash of salt and pepper, mix well, then pour into bowls and add a dollop of soured cream.

sweetcorn chowder

This deliciously creamy and luxurious soup is just the thing to warm you up on a cold night. Simply brilliant!

1 Melt the butter in a large saucepan, then add the onion and garlic and fry over a gentle heat until soft. Add the potato and cook for a few minutes. Add the milk, stock, salt and pepper and bring to the boil. Turn down the heat so the soup is simmering and cook for 10–15 minutes.

2 Add the sweetcorn, bring back to the boil and simmer for another 10–15 minutes.

3 Pour three-quarters of the soup into a blender or food processor and blend until smooth. Add to the soup left in the pan and bring back to the boil again.

4 Add more salt and pepper if it needs it, then stir in the cream and lime juice, adding a little extra stock if it is too thick. Heat the chowder until it just starts to boil then stir in the chives. Dish up straight away.

PREP

15

COOK

30

SERVES

6

mates

posh

share

50 g (2 oz) **butter**

1 large **onion**, cut into small cubes

3 **garlic cloves**, finely chopped

125 g (4 oz) **potatoes**, cut into small cubes

300 ml (½ pint) **milk**

600 ml (1 pint) **vegetable stock**

750 g (1½ lb) fresh or frozen **sweetcorn kernels** or 2 × 340 g (11½ oz) cans sweetcorn kernels, drained

65 ml (2⅛ fl oz) **single cream**

2 teaspoons **lime juice**

2 tablespoons chopped **chives**

salt and **pepper**

1 tablespoon **vegetable oil**

1 **onion**, chopped

500 g (1 lb) **mushrooms**, finely chopped

600 ml (1 pint) **vegetable stock**

1 tablespoon chopped **parsley**

2 teaspoons **cornflour**

150 ml (¼ pint) **single cream**

salt and **pepper**

PREP

COOK

30

SERVES

4

pals

party

sexy

cream of mushroom soup

Definitely one to impress your friends with! If you want to jazz it up even more then add some white wine or sherry just before the end of cooking.

1 Heat the oil in a large saucepan and cook the onion over a medium heat for about 5 minutes until soft. Add the mushrooms and cook, stirring, for 3–4 minutes.

2 Stir in the stock, parsley and salt and pepper, then bring to the boil, cover and simmer gently for 15 minutes.

3 In a small bowl mix the cornflour with a little cold water and stir into the soup, cooking for 2–3 minutes until it has thickened. Stir in the cream and serve at once.

courgette soup with basil

This soup is utterly delicious, so make sure that you aren't in a rush and have time to enjoy it properly.

1 Heat the oil and half the butter in a large saucepan. Fry the onion over a low heat until golden but not brown. Add the courgettes, mix well and fry over a low heat for about 10 minutes.

2 Add the potatoes and fry over a medium heat for 3–4 minutes, stirring well, then add the stock. Bring to the boil, cover and simmer for 40 minutes. Pour into a blender or food processor and blend until smooth.

3 In a bowl mix together the basil with the garlic, eggs, the rest of the butter and the Parmesan, then beat thoroughly until well mixed. Trickle the soup into the egg mixture and add a good dash of salt and pepper. Pour the soup back into the pan and reheat.

4 Dish up the soup and sprinkle with extra grated Parmesan if you want, then eat straight away.

PREP

10

COOK

60

SERVES

6

best

feast

yum!

4 tablespoons **vegetable oil**

25 g (1 oz) **butter**, softened

1 large **onion**, finely chopped

750 g (1½ lb) **courgettes**, sliced

2 **potatoes**, cut into cubes

1.5 litres (2½ pints) **vegetable stock**

2 tablespoons chopped **basil**

1 **garlic clove**, finely chopped

2 **eggs**

25 g (1 oz) **Parmesan cheese**, grated

salt and **pepper**

2 tablespoons **vegetable oil**

1 **apple**, peeled, cored and chopped

1 large **carrot**, chopped

25 g (1 oz) **plain flour**

1 tablespoon **curry powder**

1.2 litres (2 pints) **vegetable stock**

1 tablespoon **mango chutney**

25 g (1 oz) **sultanas**

pinch of **sugar**

2 teaspoons **lemon juice** or **wine**

salt and **pepper**

mulligatawny soup

A classic, this spicy soup is best served with poppadoms or naan bread.

spicy

tangy

great

1 Heat the oil in a large saucepan and fry the apple and carrot until soft. Stir in the flour and curry powder to make a paste. Gradually stir in the stock, bring to the boil and cook until the soup thickens.

2 Add the chutney, sultanas, sugar, a little salt and pepper and the lemon juice or wine. Cook very gently for between 45–60 minutes or until the vegetables are very soft.

3 Cool slightly then blend until smooth in a blender or food processor. Pour the soup back into the saucepan and add more salt and pepper if it needs it. Reheat the soup then pour into bowls and eat while hot.

butternut squash soup

Butternut squash has a lovely sweet taste and is delicious roasted, baked or boiled. You can spice up this soup by adding a chilli or two … depending on your tolerance.

1 Cut the squash in half and remove all the seeds. Peel off the skin and chop up the flesh into small cubes.

2 Heat the butter and oil in a large saucepan, add the onion, garlic and squash and fry for 5 minutes. Add the stock, bring to the boil and simmer for 15 minutes.

3 Pour the soup into a blender or food processor and blend until smooth. Add a good dash of salt and pepper then pour back into the saucepan and reheat gently.

4 Pour into bowls and add a generous spoonful of grated Parmesan, then dish up with a crusty roll.

PREP

5

COOK

25

SERVES

4

tasty

easy

beer

1 **butternut squash**, weighing about 875 g (1¾ lb)

50 g (2 oz) **butter**

2 tablespoons **vegetable oil**

2 **onions**, chopped

1 **garlic clove**, crushed and chopped

1 litre (1¾ pints) **vegetable stock**

salt and **pepper**

75 g (3 oz) **Parmesan cheese**, grated

bortsch

4 **beetroot**

4 **tomatoes**, skinned and chopped

1.2 litres (2 pints) **vegetable stock**

3 large **cabbage** leaves, shredded coarsely

1 **bay leaf**

½ teaspoon **caraway seeds**

6 crushed black **peppercorns**

5 tablespoons **red wine vinegar**

2 tablespoons **sugar**

6 small **potatoes**

salt

6 teaspoons **soured cream**

PREP

COOK

SERVES

smart

posh

pals

This tangy beetroot soup is perfect on a cold winter's night, so invite a few friends round, pile up a mound of fresh, crusty bread and serve this stunning purple soup in a huge pan.

1 Put the beetroot in a saucepan, cover with plenty of cold water and add 1 tablespoon of salt. Bring to the boil, turn down the heat, cover and simmer gently for 35–45 minutes. Drain off the liquid, then rinse the beetroot under cold water, dry with kitchen paper and, when cool, remove the skins.

2 Grate the beetroot into a large saucepan. Add the tomatoes, stock, cabbage, 2 teaspoons of salt, bay leaf, caraway seeds, peppercorns, vinegar and sugar. Stir well. Bring the mixture to the boil, turn down the heat, cover and simmer gently for 30 minutes.

3 Remove and chuck out the bay leaf. Drop the potatoes into the soup and continue simmering until the potatoes are tender but not too soft. Pour into bowls and top with a dollop of soured cream.

curried lentil soup

PREP

15

COOK

40

SERVES

2

If you don't have red lentils in your store cupboard then you can use yellow instead – neither type need presoaking, but don't forget to rinse them.

1 Heat the oil in large saucepan, add the onion and cook over a medium heat for 5 minutes, or until the onion softens. Add the garlic, potato, carrot, celery and curry paste and cook, stirring occasionally, for another 5 minutes.

2 Add the lentils, tomatoes, stock, salt and pepper and bring to the boil. Turn down the heat, cover and simmer for 30 minutes, or until the lentils are soft. Serve with a hunk of warm brown bread.

spicy

fab!

fun

1 tablespoon **vegetable oil**

1 small **onion**, finely chopped

1 **garlic clove**, crushed

1 small **potato**, cut into small cubes

1 **carrot**, cut into small cubes

2 **celery sticks**, finely chopped

1 tablespoon mild **curry paste**

50 g (2 oz) **red lentils**, rinsed

200 g (7 oz) can chopped **tomatoes**

600 ml (1 pint) **vegetable stock**

salt and **pepper**

50 g (2 oz) **butter**

1 **onion**, chopped

1 **celery stick**, sliced

1 large **cauliflower**, about 750 g (1½ lb), cut into small florets

900 ml (1½ pints) **vegetable stock**

900 ml (1½ pints) **milk**

1 teaspoon grated **nutmeg**

1 tablespoon **cornflour**

salt and **pepper**

15

35

SERVES

6

mates

share

telly

cauliflower soup

Cauliflower is a very versatile vegetable and makes fantastic soups. You can try adding cheeses, such as Cheddar or Stilton, to adapt this recipe.

1 Melt the butter in a large saucepan and add the onion, celery and cauliflower. Cook, covered, for 5–8 minutes over a medium heat stirring often. Stir in the stock with 450 ml (¾ pint) of the milk.

2 Bring to the boil, then turn down the heat and simmer, covered, for 25 minutes.

3 In a blender or food processor blend the mixture until smooth. Pour back into the saucepan and stir in 300 ml (½ pint) of the milk. Add a good dash of salt and pepper and stir in the nutmeg.

4 In a small bowl dissolve the cornflour in the rest of the milk, then add it to the cauliflower mixture. Bring to the boil, stirring constantly, then turn down the heat and simmer for 2 minutes. Serve with a little cream stirred in if you like it.

smooth red bean soup

A very hearty, nutritious yet tasty soup – it's an ideal way to fill up when you're on a tight budget.

1 Heat the oil in a saucepan and gently fry the onion, garlic, pepper and carrot for 3–5 minutes, stirring constantly. Add the cayenne, chilli powder, thyme, bay leaf and rosemary. Stir well then pour in the stock and water.

2 Add the beans, tomato purée and tomatoes, stirring well so the tomatoes break up. Bring the mixture to the boil, then turn down the heat and simmer, partially covered, for 1¼ hours. Stir occasionally, skimming off any froth on the surface. Remove the bay leaf.

3 Pour the mixture into a blender or food processor and blend until smooth. Sieve into a clean pan and add a good dash of salt. If the soup is too thick add a little water. Stir and heat thoroughly without allowing it to boil, then dish up straight away.

PREP

15

COOK

75

SERVES

6

tasty

great

juicy

3 tablespoons **vegetable oil**

1 **onion**, chopped

2 **garlic cloves**, chopped

1 **red pepper**, cored, deseeded and chopped

1 **carrot**, chopped

¼ teaspoon **cayenne pepper**

1 teaspoon **chilli powder**

¼ teaspoon dried **thyme**

1 **bay leaf**

¼ teaspoon dried **rosemary**

600 ml (1 pint) **vegetable stock**

1.2 litres (2 pints) **water**

250 g (8 oz) can **red kidney beans**, drained and rinsed

2 tablespoons **tomato purée**

400 g (13 oz) can peeled **plum tomatoes**

salt

300 g (10 oz) **pasta twists**

2 **spring onions**, chopped diagonally

1 **red pepper**, cored, deseeded and chopped

125 g (4 oz) canned **red kidney beans**, drained and rinsed

200 g (7 oz) canned **pinto beans**, drained and rinsed

125 g (4 oz) canned **borlotti beans**, drained and rinsed

200 ml (7 fl oz) **crème fraîche**

4 tablespoons **milk**

3 tablespoons chopped **dill**

salt and **pepper**

PREP

COOK

SERVES

fills

fab!

cheap

three bean pasta salad

A truly yummy and comforting salad – this is one you can easily adapt by adding any other ingredients you fancy.

1 Cook the pasta according to the packet instructions, until just tender. Drain, rinse under cold water, drain again and put in a large bowl.

2 Add the spring onions, pepper and beans and mix well.

3 Beat the crème fraîche and milk together in a bowl, mix into the salad and add a dash of salt and pepper.

4 Fold in the dill, sprinkle with pepper and tuck in.

potato salad

This makes a great side salad and can be livened up by adding strips of pimiento and sprinkling chopped herbs, such as chives, over the top.

COOK

SERVES

mates

beer

share

1 Cook the potatoes, whole and in their skins, in a large saucepan of boiling water for 10–15 minutes or until tender. Drain and rinse under cold water, then drain again and leave to cool.

2 Thickly slice the potatoes and place in a bowl with the spring onions and dill pickle. Add a good dash of salt and pepper.

3 To make the dressing, mix together the mayonnaise, cream and mustard in a small bowl. Spoon the dressing over the potatoes and toss well to mix, then eat while still warm.

750 g (1½ lb) waxy **potatoes**, scrubbed

4 **spring onions**, finely chopped

1 **dill pickle**, finely sliced

salt and **pepper**

Dressing:

6 tablespoons **mayonnaise**

3 tablespoons **single cream**

1 teaspoon **Dijon mustard**

500g (1 lb) **tomatoes**

175 g (6 oz) **feta cheese**, cut into cubes

½ **red onion**

16 **black olives**

handful of **parsley** leaves

1½ tablespoons **lemon juice**

3 tablespoons **olive oil**

salt and **pepper**

rustic greek salad

COOK

0

The perfect way to bring back happy memories of a summer holiday.

SERVES

6

1 If you're using large tomatoes, cut them in half lengthways, then cut each half into 3 wedges. If you're using baby tomatoes, simply cut them in half lengthways. Put them into a large bowl with the feta.

2 Cut the onion into quarters, then cut each quarter into 4 sections. Scatter the onion over the tomatoes and cheese and add the olives and parsley.

3 Pour over the lemon juice and toss very gently. Pour over the oil and toss very gently again, then sprinkle with salt and pepper. Enjoy with warm pitta bread.

fresh

fast

sexy

tabbouleh

Tabbouleh is a delicious Middle Eastern salad dish that has become a popular choice worldwide. Why not try making some Nut Koftas (see page 85) or Falafel (see page 84) to go with it?

COOK

0

175 g (6 oz) **bulgar wheat**

300 ml (½ pint) **boiling water**

1 **red onion**, finely chopped

3 **tomatoes**, cut into cubes

¼ **cucumber**, chopped

10 tablespoons chopped **parsley**

5 tablespoons chopped **mint**

SERVES

6

1 Put the bulgar wheat in a large bowl. Pour over the boiling water and leave to stand for 45–60 minutes or until the grains swell and soften.

2 Drain the wheat and press well to remove any excess water. Put in a large bowl and add the onion, tomatoes, cucumber, parsley and mint. Toss well to mix together.

3 To make the dressing, put the ingredients in a screw-top jar, replace the lid and shake until mixed. Pour over the salad and toss well, then serve straight away with pitta bread.

Dressing:

100 ml (3½ fl oz) **lemon juice**

2 teaspoons **olive oil**

black pepper

fancy

tasty

* + 45–60 minutes standing time

cool

4 tablespoons **olive oil**

2 **red onions**, thinly sliced

2 **garlic cloves**, thinly sliced

500 g (1 lb) fresh **spinach and ricotta ravioli**

375 g (12 oz) cooked **beetroot** in natural juices, drained and cut into cubes

2 tablespoons **capers**, drained and rinsed

2 tablespoons **balsamic vinegar**

a few mixed **salad leaves**

Parmesan cheese shavings

PREP

10

COOK

12

SERVES

4

posh

mates

fresh

warm ravioli salad with beetroot

Make sure you buy good-quality fresh pasta – you will find it's worth spending a bit more than usual. If you don't fancy spinach and ricotta, use any other kind of fresh ravioli.

1 Heat 1 tablespoon of the oil in a large frying pan and fry the onions and garlic over a medium heat for 10 minutes until they are softened and golden.

2 Meanwhile, cook the pasta according to the packet instructions. Drain and toss with the remaining oil.

3 Add the beetroot to the onions with the capers and vinegar and heat through. Stir into the ravioli then pour into a large bowl with all the juices from the pan. Leave to cool for 5 minutes.

4 Make a bed of salad leaves on each plate, then top with the ravioli and Parmesan shavings and enjoy.

panzanella

This classic Italian salad is a colourful combination of tomatoes, black olives, hard-boiled eggs and golden croûtons. If you don't like olives, use asparagus tips instead.

1 Heat the oven to 200°C (400°F), Gas Mark 6.

2 Put the eggs into a saucepan of water, bring to the boil and cook for 10 minutes until hard-boiled. Drain, rinse under cold water then leave to cool.

3 Meanwhile, put the cubes of bread into a small plastic bag with the oil and toss together. Tip on to a baking sheet and bake in the oven for 8–10 minutes until crisp and golden.

4 Put the tomatoes, olives and sun-dried tomatoes into a large bowl. Add the vinegar and basil and salt and pepper, then toss together well.

5 Peel the eggs, cut them into wedges and add to the salad with the warm croûtons. Eat straight away.

PREP

10

COOK

10

SERVES

2

great

yum!

feast

2 **eggs**

300 g (10 oz) **tomatoes**, cut into wedges

6 **black olives**

2 **sun-dried tomatoes** in oil, drained and thinly sliced

salt and **pepper**

Croûtons:

1 small crusty **sesame roll**, cut into cubes

2 tablespoons **olive oil**

Dressing:

1 tablespoon **balsamic vinegar**

a few torn **basil** leaves

2 teaspoons **vegetable oil**

2 **onions**, finely chopped

2 teaspoons **curry powder**

150 ml (¼ pint) natural **yogurt**

1 tablespoon **lemon juice**

40 g (1½ oz) canned **butter beans**, drained and rinsed

½ **lettuce**

salt and **pepper**

hot

spicy

beer

curried butter bean salad

If you want a stronger curry taste then simply add more curry powder. Butter beans are a good source of protein, which can be lacking in vegetarian diets.

1 Heat the oil in a large saucepan, add the onions and fry gently for 8 minutes, then add the curry powder and cook for another 2 minutes. Take off the heat and leave to cool.

2 Mix the yogurt with the lemon juice and sprinkle with salt and pepper. Add to the onion mixture, then stir in the butter beans.

3 Make a bed of lettuce on each plate, then dollop the butter bean mixture on top and tuck in.

marinated mixed pepper salad

This stunning salad has a great combination of vibrant colours. You can also add olives or capers at the end if you fancy them.

1 Make the marinade. Crush the garlic to a smooth paste with a little salt. Add the oil, vinegar, coriander, sugar and pepper and mix well.

2 Place the peppers under a moderate grill, skin sides up. Cook until the skins blister, then remove from the heat, leave to cool slightly and peel. Cut the peppers into thick strips and arrange, alternating the colours, on a large plate.

3 Spoon the marinade over the peppers, then cover loosely with clingfilm. Leave in a cool place for at least 30 minutes then enjoy.

PREP

15

COOK

5

SERVES

4

posh

star

tangy

1 **red pepper**, cored, deseeded and halved

1 **green pepper**, cored, deseeded and halved

1 **yellow pepper**, cored, deseeded and halved

Marinade:

1 **garlic clove**

6 tablespoons **vegetable oil**

3 tablespoons **wine vinegar**

¼ teaspoon ground **coriander**

1 teaspoon **sugar**

salt and **pepper**

cheap eats

1 **courgette**, sliced

1 **aubergine**, cut into cubes

5 **cherry tomatoes**, halved

1 teaspoon **olive oil**

2 **mini baguettes**

75 g (3 oz) **goats' cheese**, sliced

tasty

easy

gooey

roasted vegetable baguette

A fantastic sarnie! You can also use roasted peppers, which will add even more colour to your sandwich, or try adding sun-dried tomatoes for a different taste.

1 Heat the oven to 180°C (350°F), Gas Mark 4.

2 Spread out all the vegetables on a large baking sheet and drizzle with the olive oil.

3 Bake for about 40 minutes, turning occasionally until nicely roasted. Pop the baguettes into the oven on a low shelf to warm for the last 5 minutes.

4 Cut the baguettes in half and dollop a large spoonful of the roasted vegetables on to each one. Top with the sliced goats' cheese, close and tuck in.

avocado, mozzarella and tomato ciabatta

Avocado, tomato and mozzarella work together superbly, and the warm, gooey cheese is just so moreish that you'll be making this sandwich again and again.

PREP

5

COOK

12

SERVES

2

juicy

mates

sexy

2 **ciabatta rolls**

1 large or 2 small **avocados**, sliced

50 g (2 oz) **mozzarella cheese**, sliced thinly

2 large **tomatoes**, sliced

1 tablespoon roughly chopped **basil**

black pepper

1 Heat the oven to 180°C (350°F), Gas Mark 4.

2 Heat the ciabatta in the oven for about 10 minutes.

3 Layer the avocado, mozzarella and tomatoes on the warm rolls, add the basil and sprinkle with pepper. Pop the rolls back into the oven for 2–3 minutes so the mozzarella goes really gooey, then eat straight away.

greek wrap

75 g (3 oz) **feta cheese**

2 **tortillas**

2 **tomatoes**, sliced

½ **red onion**, finely sliced

10 **black olives**, pitted
and cut in half

handful of **baby spinach**
leaves

drizzle of **olive oil**

PREP

5

COOK

0

SERVES

2

yum!

fast

great

Really simple and quick to make, this is so delightfully fresh-tasting that it is perfect for lunch on a warm summer's day.

1 Crumble the feta on to the tortillas. Add the tomato, red onion, olives and spinach leaves, then drizzle with olive oil.

2 Wrap the tortillas round the filling and eat immediately.

artichoke pittas

Fast food doesn't have to be unhealthy, as this delicious sandwich – which takes only 5 minutes to make – proves.

1 Mix the sun-dried tomatoes, artichoke hearts, goats' cheese and chillies in a large bowl with a dash of olive oil.

2 Generously stuff the pitta breads and sprinkle with black pepper – an instant lunch!

PREP

5

COOK

0

SERVES

2

quick

snack

fab

10 **sun-dried tomatoes** in oil, drained and chopped

425 g (14 oz) can **artichoke hearts**, drained and chopped

75 g (3 oz) crumbly **goats' cheese**

4 chopped sweet **pimiento chillies**

olive oil

2 **pitta breads**, toasted

black pepper

2 **tomatoes**, sliced

lettuce leaves

100 g (3 ½ oz) **Cheddar cheese**, sliced thinly

6 thick slices **granary bread**, buttered

3 tablespoons **pickle** or **chutney**

pepper

PREP

5

COOK

0

SERVES

2

super

pals

beer

double-decker ploughman's

This super sandwich will really put an end to those revision hunger pangs and can be adapted to suit whatever you can find in your fridge.

1 Layer half the tomato and lettuce and a quarter of the cheese on a slice of bread and sprinkle with pepper.

2 Spread a slice of bread with pickle or chutney and place on top. Then add another layer of cheese and another of pickle before finishing with the final slice of bread. Repeat to make the other sandwich, then tuck in.

classic egg and cress sandwich

Egg mayonnaise and cress on white bread is one of the all-time great comfort foods – just make sure that the bread is really fresh, and that you add a good dash of salt and pepper to season the egg mayo.

1 Boil a saucepan of water then carefully add the eggs to the pan using a spoon so they do not crack. Boil for 8–10 minutes, run under cold water, then leave to cool.

2 Chop up the eggs and mix well in a bowl with the mayonnaise, cress, a few drops of Worcestershire sauce and a good sprinkling of salt and pepper.

3 Pile the mixture on to 2 slices of the bread, then top with the rest of the bread. Delicious!

PREP

COOK

SERVES

cheap

fills

star

2 **eggs**

2 tablespoons **mayonnaise**

1 handful of **cress**

vegetarian **Worcestershire sauce**

4 slices **white bread**, buttered

salt and **pepper**

1 **aubergine**, sliced into
1 cm (½ inch) pieces

1 **onion**, thinly sliced

olive oil

2 tablespoons **Hummus**
(see page 100)

2 or 4 thick slices
sun-dried tomato bread

black pepper

2

fun

hot

feast

aubergine and hummus sandwich

Make this into a proper 'doorstep' by cutting thick hunks of the sun-dried tomato bread. This should not be a dainty sarnie!

1 Heat the oven to 180°C (350°F), Gas Mark 4.

2 Spread out the aubergine and the onion on a large baking sheet with a little olive oil and roast in the oven until soft, which should take about 40 minutes.

3 Spread the hummus thickly on to the tomato bread, spoon on the roasted aubergine and top with the onions. Sprinkle with pepper and eat as an open sandwich or top with another hunk of bread.

super salad sandwich with lemon mayo

The tangy lemon mayonnaise really livens up this very healthy sandwich. If you want to try something slightly different use lime juice instead of the lemon.

1 First make the lemon mayo by mixing the ingredients together well in a small bowl. Spread on to the inside of the wholemeal rolls.

2 Pile the salad vegetables and carrot into the rolls, sprinkle with salt and pepper and enjoy.

PREP

5

COOK

0

SERVES

2

tangy

mates

telly

2 **wholemeal rolls**, cut in half

2 handfuls of mixed **salad leaves**

2 **tomatoes**, sliced

1 **red pepper**, cored, deseeded and sliced

1 **avocado**, sliced

1 **carrot**, grated

salt and **pepper**

Lemon mayo:

2 tablespoons **mayonnaise**

1 teaspoon **lemon juice**

10 **basil** leaves, chopped

vegetable fajitas

2 tablespoons **vegetable oil**

2 large **onions**, thinly sliced

2 **garlic cloves**, crushed

2 **red peppers**, cored, deseeded and thinly sliced

2 **green peppers**, cored, deseeded and thinly sliced

4 **green chillies**, deseeded and thinly sliced

2 teaspoons chopped **oregano**

250 g (8 oz) **button mushrooms**, sliced

12 **tortillas**

salt and **pepper**

To top:

Tomato salsa (see page 103)

Guacamole (see page 105)

soured cream

PREP

15

COOK

15

SERVES

4

party

fun

beer

These Mexican wraps are great to have at a party, as people can make up their own. They are the ideal beer food.

1 Heat the oil in a large frying pan and fry the onions and garlic for about 5 minutes until they are soft and golden brown.

2 Add the red and green peppers, chillies and oregano and stir well. Fry gently for about 10 minutes until cooked and tender.

3 Add the mushrooms and cook quickly for 1 minute more, stirring well to mix the mushrooms with the other vegetables. Add a good dash of salt and pepper and stir again.

4 Spoon the sizzling hot vegetables into the tortillas and add whatever toppings you like. Roll up or fold over the fajita, then bite in!

quesadillas

PREP

15

COOK

10

SERVES

4

Carry on the Mexican theme with tequila shots or some exotic cocktails – a great ice-breaker.

1 Divide the refried beans among the tortillas, putting a spoonful of mixture on one half of each tortilla, leaving a little space around the edge.

2 Dollop some cheese on top of the beans and then add a few slices of chilli. Fold the tortilla over the top of the filling.

3 Press the edges of each folded tortilla firmly between your fingertips. It helps if the tortillas are soft and quite damp when you do this.

4 Pour a good glug of oil into a large, deep frying pan to a depth of about 4 cm (1½ inches) and heat until hot. Fry the quesadillas, in batches, until crisp and golden brown. Remove and drain on kitchen paper. Serve hot with salsa, guacamole and soured cream.

crisp

green

saucy

175 g (6 oz) canned **refried beans**

12 **tortillas**

175 g (6 oz) **Cheddar cheese**, grated

175 g (6 oz) **mozzarella cheese**, cut into strips

4–6 **green chillies**, deseeded and thinly sliced

vegetable oil, for frying

To top:

Tomato salsa (see page 103)

Guacamole (see page 105)

soured cream

6 large **courgettes**

275 g (9 oz) frozen **sweetcorn kernels**, thawed

2 **garlic cloves**, crushed

2 **eggs**

2 tablespoons **milk**

175 g (6 oz) **feta cheese**, rinsed and crumbled

25 g (1 oz) **butter**, melted

salt and **pepper**

PREP

10*

COOK

40

SERVES

6

cool

smart

yum!

mexican courgettes

This tasty bake just needs a crisp green salad and an even crisper glass of white wine to accompany it to make the perfect meal.

1 Halve the courgettes lengthways. Using a teaspoon, carefully scoop out the flesh to leave a 1 cm (½ inch) shell. Sprinkle salt inside the courgettes and leave them upside down to drain for 1 hour.

2 Carefully wipe the insides of the courgettes with kitchen paper to remove the salt. Put into a shallow ovenproof dish.

3 Heat the oven to 180°C (350°F), Gas Mark 4.

4 Blend the sweetcorn, garlic, eggs, milk and pepper to a coarse consistency in a blender or food processor. Add 125 g (4 oz) of the feta then the mixture divide among the courgette shells. Scatter over the rest of the cheese and trickle over the butter. Bake in the oven for 30–40 minutes until the courgettes are tender and the tops lightly browned; cover with foil if they brown too quickly. Eat hot with a green salad or crusty bread.

* + draining

black bean chilli

The chilli takes a while to make, but it's worth it! It's a great meal to dish up for friends as even hardened carnivores will love it.

1 Drain and rinse the beans, then place them in a large saucepan with the water. Bring to the boil and boil rapidly for 10 minutes. Turn down the heat, cover and simmer for 45 minutes.

2 Heat half the oil in a frying pan and fry the mushrooms for 5 minutes. Remove the mushrooms from the pan and put them in a bowl.

3 Add the rest of the oil to the pan and fry the onion, garlic, potato, pepper and spices over a medium heat for 10 minutes.

4 Drain the beans, keeping the liquid. Return the liquid to the saucepan and boil until it has reduced to 450 ml (¾ pint). Stir the beans into the frying pan with the vegetables and add the reduced liquid, passata and mushrooms. Bring to the boil, cover and simmer for 30 minutes.

5 Stir in the lime juice and coriander, then cook for another 5 minutes. Delicious with boiled rice.

PREP

20*

COOK

105

SERVES

8

pals

boozy

party

250 g (8 oz) dried **black kidney beans**, soaked overnight

1.5 litres (2½ pints) **water**

4 tablespoons **vegetable oil**

250 g (8 oz) small **mushrooms**, halved

1 large **onion**, chopped

2 **garlic cloves**, crushed

2 large **potatoes**, cut into cubes

1 **red** or **green pepper**, cored, deseeded and cut into cubes

2 teaspoons ground **coriander**

1 teaspoon ground **cumin**

2 teaspoons hot **chilli powder**

450 ml (¾ pint) **passata**

1 tablespoon **lime juice**

2 tablespoons chopped **coriander**

4 **carrots**, thickly sliced diagonally

250 g (8 oz) **swede**, cut into cubes

250 g (8 oz) **sweet potato**, cut into cubes

1 **onion**, cut into 8 wedges

2 **leeks**, thickly sliced diagonally

6 **garlic cloves**

½ teaspoon **mustard** or **cumin seeds**, lightly crushed

½ teaspoon **coriander seeds**, lightly crushed

2 cm (1 inch) piece fresh **root ginger**, peeled and finely grated

1 tablespoon **olive oil**

100 ml (3½ fl oz) **white wine**

black pepper

fills

good

feast

spiced root vegetables

Serve with a nut roast for a traditional Sunday lunch – although it's easily filling enough to make a great meal on its own.

1 Heat the oven to 200°C (400°F), Gas Mark 6.

2 Put all the vegetables and the garlic in a large roasting tin. Sprinkle over the crushed seeds and squeeze over the ginger pulp so the juice comes out. Sprinkle with pepper and drizzle over the oil.

3 Roast in the oven for 30 minutes, stirring occasionally.

4 Pour over the wine and bake for another 10 minutes, then eat while hot and crunchy.

spicy bean burgers

Sometimes only a burger will do – and this will certainly set you up for a night of partying.

1 To make the tzatziki, slice the cucumber in half lengthways and use a teaspoon to remove the seeds. Cut the flesh into cubes then stir with the garlic into the yogurt and sprinkle with salt and pepper.

2 Heat the oil in a frying pan, add the celery, onion, garlic, chilli and ginger and fry over a medium heat for 5 minutes or until soft.

3 Drain the beans, then rinse and drain again. Place in a food processor or blender and blend until almost smooth. Add the onion mixture, cumin, coriander and salt and pepper. Mix together well then lightly flour your hands and make 6 burgers out of the mixture. Cover and refrigerate for 30 minutes.

4 Heat the oven to 200°C (400°F), Gas Mark 6.

5 Dip the burgers into the egg, then coat in breadcrumbs. Place on a baking sheet and cook in the oven for 20 minutes.

6 Cut the rolls in half, top with the burgers and a good dollop of tzatziki and tuck in.

PREP

20*

COOK

25

SERVES

6

tasty

cool

fab!

1 tablespoon **olive oil**

2 **celery sticks**, chopped

1 large **red onion**, finely chopped

1 large **garlic clove**, crushed

1 small **red chilli**, deseeded and finely chopped

2.5 cm (1 inch) piece of fresh **root ginger**, peeled and finely grated

875 g (1¾ lb) canned **mixed beans**

1 teaspoon ground **cumin**

2 tablespoons chopped **coriander**

plain flour, for dusting

1 **egg**, beaten

100 g (3½ oz) **breadcrumbs**

6 **burger rolls**

salt and **pepper**

Tzatziki:

½ **cucumber**

1 **garlic clove**, crushed

200 ml (7 fl oz) **plain yogurt**

425 g (14 oz) can **chickpeas**, rinsed and drained

1 **onion**, roughly chopped

3 **garlic cloves**, roughly chopped

2 teaspoons **cumin** seeds

1 teaspoon mild **chilli powder**

2 tablespoons chopped **mint**

3 tablespoons chopped **coriander**

50 g (2 oz) **breadcrumbs**

vegetable oil, for frying

salt and **pepper**

best

great

fun

falafel

These spicy chickpea cakes make a great veggie supper served simply with a Rustic Greek Salad (see page 60).

1 Put the chickpeas in a blender or food processor with the onion, garlic, spices, herbs, breadcrumbs and a little salt and pepper. Blend to make a chunky paste.

2 Take dessertspoonfuls of the mixture and flatten into round cakes.

3 Heat oil to a 1 cm (½ inch) depth in a frying pan and fry half the falafel for about 3 minutes, turning once, until crisp and golden. Drain on kitchen paper and keep warm while you cook the rest of the falafel.

nut koftas with minted yogurt

20

COOK

10

SERVES

4

green

mates

share

The crunchiness of the nut koftas and the creaminess and tanginess of the minty yogurt complement each other perfectly. Best served with naan bread.

1 Heat 3 tablespoons of the oil in a frying pan, add the onion and fry for 4 minutes. Add the chilli flakes, garlic and curry paste and fry for another minute.

2 Pour into a blender or food processor with the beans, ground and chopped almonds, egg and a little salt and pepper and blend until the mixture starts to stick together.

3 Put a little flour on your hands, take about one-eighth of the mixture and mould it around a skewer, forming it into a sausage about 2.5 cm (1 inch) thick. Make 7 more koftas in the same way.

4 Brush the koftas with the remaining oil. Grill under a moderate grill for about 5 minutes until golden, turning once.

5 Meanwhile, make the minted yogurt. Mix together the yogurt and mint in a small bowl. In a separate bowl, make the lemon dressing by mixing together the oil with the lemon juice and a little salt and pepper.

6 Brush the koftas with the lemon dressing, dollop on the minted yogurt and tuck in.

4 tablespoons **vegetable oil**

1 **onion**, chopped

½ teaspoon **chilli flakes**

2 **garlic cloves**, chopped

1 tablespoon **curry paste**

425 g (14 oz) can **cannellini beans**, rinsed and drained

125 g (4 oz) **ground almonds**

75 g (3 oz) **chopped almonds**

1 small **egg**

plain flour, for dusting

salt and **pepper**

8 wooden **skewers**

Minted yogurt:

200 ml (7 fl oz) **Greek yogurt**

2 tablespoons chopped **mint**

Lemon dressing:

2 tablespoons **vegetable oil**

1 tablespoon **lemon juice**

cheesy clouds

150 g (5 oz) **broccoli** florets

40 g (1½ oz) **butter**

1 tablespoon grated **Parmesan cheese**

3 **eggs**

25 g (1 oz) **plain flour**

150 ml (¼ pint) **milk**

100 g (3½ oz) **Cheddar cheese**, grated

1 teaspoon **mustard**

pinch of **cayenne pepper**

PREP

COOK

SERVES

light

moist

sexy

These light and airy cheese soufflés conceal a surprise layer of broccoli, although you can add cauliflower or leeks if you prefer.

1 Heat the oven to 190°C (375°F), Gas Mark 5.

2 In a saucepan bring water to the boil then add the broccoli and boil for 3–4 minutes or until just tender. Meanwhile, grease 4 small 200 ml (7 fl oz) dishes or similar with a little of the butter, then sprinkle with the Parmesan.

3 Crack the eggs, carefully separating the yolks from the whites into 2 bowls.

4 Melt the rest of the butter in a saucepan, stir in the flour and cook for 1 minute. Gradually stir in the milk and bring to the boil, stirring until thick, smooth and lump-free. Take the pan off the heat and stir in the cheese, mustard and cayenne. Gradually beat in the egg yolks, one at a time.

5 Whisk the egg whites in a bowl until soft, moist peaks form. Stir a little of the egg white into the cheese mixture to lighten it, then carefully fold in the rest.

6 Share out the broccoli among the 4 dishes, then pour the cheese mixture over the top. Bake in the oven for 15 minutes then dish up. Delicious with cherry tomatoes and toast.

quick veggie pasties

Pasties are ideal hangover food – they will line your stomach and give you a much-needed energy boost.

1 Heat the oven to 200°C (400°F), Gas Mark 6.

2 Pour the flour into a large bowl and rub in the butter with your fingertips until it is mixed well. Stir in the cheese, make a hole in the centre and mix in enough water to give a soft but not sticky dough. Knead the dough lightly and divide into 4 equal pieces. Roll each one out on a lightly floured surface and cut to an 18 cm (7 inch) circle (you can use a small plate as a guide).

3 Mix together all the ingredients for the filling then divide the mixture evenly among the pasties. Lightly dampen the edges of the pastry and pull them together to meet in the centres, pressing well to seal in the filling.

4 Place on a baking sheet and cook in the oven for 20 minutes. Turn down the heat slightly and cook for another 15–20 minutes.

PREP

35

COOK

40

SERVES

4

beer

hot

share

375 g (12 oz) **plain flour**

125 g (4 oz) **butter**, softened and cut into cubes

200 g (7 oz) **Danish blue cheese**, grated

about 4 tablespoons **water**

Filling:

175 g (6 oz) **carrots**, coarsely grated

250 g (8 oz) **potatoes**, cut into cubes

175 g (6 oz) **onions**, finely chopped

25 g (1 oz) **Danish blue cheese**, grated

1½ teaspoons dried **mixed herbs**

3 tablespoons **vegetable stock**

salt and **pepper**

baked eggs

COOK

35

The gorgeously rich, paprika-red mixture of slowly cooked red peppers, tomatoes, onion and courgettes goes perfectly with the runny yolks of the eggs.

5 tablespoons **vegetable oil**

1 **onion**, sliced

4 **garlic cloves**, crushed

4 **red peppers**, cored, deseeded and sliced

1 **courgette**, sliced

5 **tomatoes**, sliced

2 tablespoons chopped **parsley**

large pinch of **paprika**

large pinch of dried **chilli flakes**

4 **eggs**

salt and **pepper**

SERVES

4

1 Heat the oil in a large frying pan then add the onion and fry until golden. Add the garlic, peppers, courgette and tomatoes and simmer for 15–20 minutes, stirring occasionally, until all the vegetables are soft.

2 Stir in the parsley, paprika and chilli flakes and add a good dash of salt and pepper. Simmer for another 5 minutes.

3 Heat the oven to 160°C (325°F), Gas Mark 3.

4 Spoon the vegetable mixture into a large ovenproof dish. Make 4 holes, spaced equally apart, in the mixture and carefully break an egg into each one.

5 Bake in the oven for 10 minutes until the egg whites are just set and the yolks are still runny, then tuck in straight away.

tangy

juicy

easy

herby corn-on-the-cob

PREP

15

COOK

35

SERVES

4

fun

star

mates

Corn-on-the-cob can be really messy to eat, but it's one of those foods that you can't possibly think about eating with a knife and fork! You just have to use your fingers.

1 Heat the oven to 200°C (400°F), Gas Mark 6.

2 Bring a large saucepan of water to the boil, add the corn cobs and cook for 15 minutes, then drain.

3 Mix together the butter with the herbs and salt and pepper. Spread a little over each corn cob then wrap each one individually in a piece of foil, pressing the edges together well to seal them.

4 Put the foil parcels on a baking sheet in the oven and cook for 20 minutes.

5 Unwrap the parcels carefully, put on a plate and pour over the herb butter. Delicious!

4 **corn cobs**, husks and silky thread removed

50 g (2 oz) **butter**

1 tablespoon chopped mixed **herbs** (such as parsley, thyme or chives)

salt and **pepper**

2 **aubergines**

2 large **courgettes**

2 large **tomatoes**

4 **field mushrooms**

1 tablespoon **vegetable oil**, plus extra for brushing

1 **garlic clove**, crushed

1 **onion**, chopped

125 g (4 oz) **mushrooms**, chopped

200 g (7 oz) **breadcrumbs**

2 tablespoons chopped **basil**

PREP

40

COOK

30

SERVES

4

stuffed vegetables

When it's wet, cold and miserable outside, this is the perfect dish to enjoy cosily indoors with a few bottles of red wine.

green

fills

juicy

1 Heat the oven to 200°C (400°F), Gas Mark 6.

2 Cut the ends off the aubergines and courgettes and halve lengthways. Hollow out the centres and cut the flesh into small pieces. Remove the stalks from the field mushrooms.

3 Boil a large saucepan of water, pop the shells in and boil for 2 minutes. Drain, leave to cool, brush with oil, inside and out, and place in two roasting tins.

4 Meanwhile, cut the tomatoes in half and scoop the flesh and seeds into a bowl. Throw away the skins.

5 Heat the oil in a frying pan and fry the garlic and onion until golden brown. Add the mushrooms, aubergine, courgette and tomato flesh, breadcrumbs and basil. Fry for a couple of minutes, mixing well, then add a dash of salt and pepper and spoon into the vegetable shells.

6 Pour 2–3 tablespoons of water into each roasting tin and bake in the oven for about 20 minutes. Eat straight away.

90 cheap eats

vegetarian cheeseburgers with chips

All you need now is ketchup ...

PREP

20

COOK

40

SERVES

4

1 Heat the oven to 220°C (425°F), Gas Mark 7.

2 To make the chips, scrub the potatoes and cut them into small wedges. Pat them dry on kitchen paper and put in a roasting tin. Drizzle with the oil and sprinkle with the spices. Roast in the oven for about 30 minutes until golden, turning once or twice.

3 Meanwhile, make the burgers. Put the beans in a large bowl and mash with a fork to break them up. Add the onion, cheese, breadcrumbs, egg and salt and pepper, and mix to a smooth paste.

4 Put a little flour on your hands, then shape the mixture into 4 burgers. Heat the oil in a frying pan and fry the burgers gently for 8–10 minutes, turning once, until crisp and golden. Serve with the jacket chips and mayo or ketchup – whatever you like!

party

beer

great

Jacket chips:

1 kg (2 lb) **baking potatoes**

3 tablespoons **vegetable oil**

1 teaspoon ground **cumin**

1 teaspoon ground **coriander**

1 teaspoon **chilli powder**

Cheeseburgers:

400 g (13 oz) can **red kidney beans**, rinsed and drained

1 small **onion**, finely chopped

100 g (3½ oz) **Cheddar cheese**, grated

100 g (3½ oz) **breadcrumbs**

1 **egg**

plain flour, for dusting

1 tablespoon **vegetable oil**

salt and **pepper**

3 large **red onions**

3 tablespoons
vegetable oil

250 g (8 oz) **mushrooms**,
roughly sliced

½ teaspoon medium
curry paste

400 g (13 oz) can
chickpeas, drained

grated rind of 1 **lemon**

75 g (3 oz) **breadcrumbs**

plain flour, for dusting

1 teaspoon **caster sugar**

salt and **pepper**

PREP

COOK

SERVES

best

telly

pals

chickpea and mushroom bangers

These delicious sausages are surprisingly quick and easy to make. Just pile on top of a mound of mashed potatoes (see page 93) and pour on a glug of vegetarian gravy. Pure comfort food.

1 Thinly slice 2 of the onions, put to one side, and roughly chop the other onion. Heat 1 tablespoon of the oil in a frying pan. Add the chopped onion and fry for 3 minutes. Add the mushrooms and fry for about 5 minutes until they are golden.

2 Pour the mixture into a blender or food processor and add the curry paste, chickpeas, lemon rind and salt and pepper. Blend to a coarse paste, then add the breadcrumbs and blend until mixed.

3 Put a little flour on your hands and shape the mixture into 10–12 sausages, then pop on to a baking sheet.

4 Heat 1 tablespoon of the oil in a frying pan. Add the sliced onions with the sugar and fry gently for 10 minutes or until golden and caramelized. Meanwhile, brush the sausages with the rest of the oil and cook under a moderate grill for about 10 minutes, turning frequently until evenly golden (do not let them burn!). Dish up with the caramelized onions. Perfect with mash or noodles or in a bun.

creamy mashed potatoes

To make really decadently luscious mash choose floury potatoes and heat the milk. Just make sure you make a huge pot of it as people are bound to want more ... and more ...

PREP

COOK

SERVES

4

easy

fab!

feast

6 **potatoes**, peeled

125–250 ml (4–8 fl oz) hot **milk**

50 g (2 oz) **butter**

salt and **pepper**

1 Cook the potatoes in a large saucepan of boiling water until they are soft, which should take about 20 minutes.

2 Drain the potatoes, then return to the saucepan and shake over a low heat for a few minutes until the potatoes are thoroughly dry. Mash with a potato masher or fork. Then, using a wooden spoon, beat until smooth.

3 Meanwhile, heat the milk in a small saucepan until hot but not boiling.

4 Add the butter to the potatoes, then gradually beat in the hot milk until the potatoes are light and fluffy. Add a good dash of salt and pepper and mix well.

Variations:

Garlic mash: Fry a couple of sliced garlic cloves in the butter until golden, then use in the mash.

Cheese mash: Either add grated Cheddar cheese to the mash and mix in well, or sprinkle over the top at the end.

2 large **baking potatoes**

15 g (½ oz) **butter**

100 g (3½ oz) **Cheddar cheese**, grated

5

75

2

super

fills

good

baked potatoes

Baked potatoes are one of the cheapest, easiest but most versatile dishes to make. Everyone has their favourite topping, but why not be a bit more adventurous and try some of the alternatives we have suggested.

1 Heat the oven to 200°C (400°F), Gas Mark 6.

2 Clean the skins of the potatoes and prick all over with a fork. Bake in the oven for about 1¼ hours until tender.

3 Cut the potatoes into quarters, add a good dollop of butter and sprinkle with cheese. Easy yet very filling.

Alternative toppings:

Herby butter

Cottage cheese and chive

Baked beans

Coleslaw

Black Bean Chilli (see page 81)

Vegetable Curry (see page 154)

champ

Champ is one of the best-known ways of serving Ireland's favourite vegetable – the potato. All you need is a pint of the black stuff to go with it.

PREP

15

COOK

25

SERVES

4

1 kg (2 lb) **potatoes**, left unpeeled

150 ml (¼ pint) **milk**

4–5 **spring onions**, finely chopped

salt and **pepper**

To top:

50–125 g (2–4 oz) **butter**

2 **spring onions**, finely chopped

1 Cook the potatoes in a large saucepan of boiling water for about 20 minutes or until tender.

2 Meanwhile, in another saucepan bring the milk and spring onions to the boil and simmer for a few minutes. Keep warm.

3 Drain the potatoes and return to the pan. Cook them over a very low heat, shaking, until they are completely dry. Then, holding the warm potatoes in a clean tea towel, peel them carefully and mash well using a potato masher or fork.

4 Gradually beat the milk into the mash to form a soft but not sloppy mixture. Beat in half the butter and add a good dash of salt and pepper.

5 Share out the champ among 4 plates and make a dip in the centre of each. Cut the rest of the butter into four pieces and pop a bit in each hole, then sprinkle with the extra spring onions. Sublime!

sexy

great

beer

1 kg (2 lb) **floury potatoes**, scrubbed but unpeeled

75 g (3 oz) **butter**

1 small **onion**, very finely chopped

salt and **pepper**

PREP

COOK

SERVES

posh

crisp

smart

rösti

This crunchy potato pancake is extremely tasty, especially when it's topped with a fried egg or tomato sauce. It's actually very easy to make a good rösti – the secret is to grate the potatoes when they are cold.

1 Cook the potatoes in a large saucepan of boiling water for about 7 minutes, then drain well. When the potatoes are completely cold, peel them and grate them coarsely into a large bowl.

2 Heat 15 g (½ oz) of the butter in a large frying pan. Add the onion and cook for about 5 minutes until soft. Stir the onion into the grated potato and sprinkle with salt and pepper. Mix well.

3 Melt the rest of the butter in the frying pan. Pour about 1 tablespoon of the melted butter into a cup. Add the potato mixture to the pan and shape it into a cake. Cook gently for about 15 minutes, or until the bottom of the cake is golden brown, shaking the pan occasionally so that the rösti does not stick.

4 To cook the top of the rösti, pour over the melted butter from the cup, turn the rösti over in the frying pan and fry on the other side until brown. Cut into wedges and eat straight away while lovely and crunchy.

garlic toast with creamy avocado

A great snack when you want to impress. If you want to liven it up even more, top with pimiento peppers or shavings of Parmesan cheese as well.

1 Heat the oven to 220°C (425°F), Gas Mark 7.

2 Mix the oil and garlic together and brush all over the top of the bread slices. Place on a baking sheet and bake for 6–8 minutes until lightly golden.

3 Meanwhile, cut the avocado in half and scoop the flesh into a bowl. Mash in the chilli, lime juice and salt and pepper until fairly smooth. Spread over the toasts, drizzle with olive oil, and eat straight away.

PREP

5

COOK

6

SERVES

4

spicy

fresh

snack

3 tablespoons **olive oil**, plus extra to drizzle

1 large **garlic clove**, crushed

6 thick slices **French stick**

1 ripe **avocado**

1 **red chilli,** deseeded and finely chopped

juice of ½ **lime**

salt and **pepper**

cheese straws

125 g (4 oz) **plain flour**

50 g (2 oz) **butter**, softened and cut into cubes

75 g (3 oz) **Cheddar cheese**, grated

1 **egg yolk**

1 **egg**, beaten

Ever popular, these are a healthier snack than crisps, and are perfect for dipping into Hummus (see page 100) or Guacamole (see page 105).

1 Heat the oven to 200°C (400°F), Gas Mark 6.

2 Put the flour in a large bowl, add the butter and rub in using your fingertips until the mixture looks like breadcrumbs. Stir in the cheese and the egg yolk along with 1 tablespoon of beaten egg. Mix until it makes a dough.

3 Spread a little flour on a work surface and knead the dough lightly, then roll out to about 1 cm (½ inch) thick. Cut into 1 × 5 cm (½ × 2 inch) strips. Brush with the rest of the beaten egg, then place the straws, slightly apart, on a baking sheet.

4 Bake in the oven for 8–10 minutes until golden, then leave to cool. A delicious snack.

vegetable crisps

These are fun to make and go really well with all kinds of alcohol – what more do you want?

1 Cut the vegetables into very thin slices with a sharp knife – make them as thin as you can. Pat them dry on kitchen paper.

2 Pour the oil into a large saucepan until about a third full. Heat the oil until a piece of vegetable sizzles on the surface. Add a batch of vegetable slices to the oil and fry until crisp and golden.

3 Carefully remove and drain on kitchen paper while you fry the rest in batches (do not add too many pieces at once or they will go soggy). Sprinkle with salt and pepper and serve with beer or wine!

PREP

10

COOK

5

SERVES

4

fancy

snack

party

250 g (8 oz) **potato**

250 g (8 oz) **parsnip**

250 g (8 oz) **beetroot**

vegetable oil, for deep-frying

salt and **pepper**

hummus

PREP

20*

COOK

90

SERVES

6

400 g (13 oz) can **chickpeas**, drained and rinsed

2–3 **garlic cloves**, crushed with a little salt

250 ml (8 fl oz) **lemon juice**

5 tablespoons **tahini**

salt

To top:

olive oil

paprika

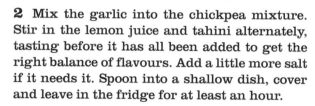

telly

moist

fresh

You can vary the amount of lemon juice and tahini that you add depending on your taste – just don't let the sesame flavour of the tahini overpower the taste of the chickpeas.

1 Put the chickpeas into a blender or food processor and blend until smooth and mushy.

2 Mix the garlic into the chickpea mixture. Stir in the lemon juice and tahini alternately, tasting before it has all been added to get the right balance of flavours. Add a little more salt if it needs it. Spoon into a shallow dish, cover and leave in the fridge for at least an hour.

3 Take the hummus out of the fridge about ½ hour before you want to eat it. Just before you serve it make swirls in the surface with the back of a spoon then trickle olive oil into the swirls and sprinkle with paprika. Delicious with olives and warm pitta bread.

* + soaking and chilling

garlic, herb and bean pâté

This takes just a few minutes to make and is best with either warm bread, Cheese Straws (see page 98) or raw vegetable sticks.

1 Put the beans, cream cheese, garlic and pesto in a blender or food processor and blend until smooth.

2 Add the spring onions and salt and pepper and blend for 10 seconds. Pour into a dish and chill until you are ready to eat it.

PREP

5

COOK

0

SERVES

4

quick

easy

posh

425 g (14 oz) can **flageolet beans**, drained and rinsed

125 g (4 oz) **cream cheese**

2 **garlic cloves**, chopped

3 tablespoons **pesto**

2 **spring onions**, chopped

salt and **pepper**

blue cheese dip

200 g (7 oz) **Danish blue cheese**

2 tablespoons **mayonnaise**

150 ml (¼ pint) **double cream**

black pepper

PREP

COOK

This moreish dip is a real palate pleaser. Soft and creamy, it's delicious with raw carrot or celery sticks – or spread it on toast for a decadent snack.

SERVES

1 Put everything into a blender or food processor and blend until smooth.

2 You can keep this dip in the fridge for a few days – if it lasts that long.

pals

gooey

yum!

guacamole with tortilla chips

The ideal party food – so invite round your friends, get out the tequila and party all night.

1 Cut the avocados in half and remove the stones. Scoop the flesh into a large bowl, add the lime juice and mash coarsely.

2 Add the garlic, spring onions, chillies, salt and pepper. Mix in the chopped tomatoes. Cover and chill in the fridge for about an hour.

3 Meanwhile, make the tortilla chips. Cut each tortilla into 8 equal pieces. Heat the oil in a saucepan so it is really hot – a cube of bread dropped into the oil should brown in 30 seconds. Add the tortilla chips and deep-fry until crisp and golden. Drain on kitchen paper and sprinkle with a little paprika and salt, then serve with the guacamole.

* + chilling

PREP

5*

COOK

5

SERVES

4

beer

party

snack

2 large **avocados**

3 tablespoons **lime juice**

2 **garlic cloves**, crushed

40 g (1½ oz) **spring onions**, chopped

1–2 **green chillies**, deseeded and chopped

125 g (4 oz) **tomatoes**, skinned, deseeded and chopped

salt and **pepper**

Tortilla chips:

8 **tortillas**

vegetable oil, for deep-frying

1 tablespoon **paprika**

viva italia

4 ready-to-cook **pizza bases**

300 g (10 oz) **mozzarella cheese**, cut into cubes

2 tablespoons **black olives**, pitted

olive oil, for brushing and drizzling

Fresh tomato sauce:

3 tablespoons **olive oil**

2 **red onions**, finely sliced

2 **garlic cloves**, crushed and chopped

2 × 400 g (13 oz) cans chopped **tomatoes**

1 teaspoon **red wine vinegar**

pinch of **sugar**

salt and **pepper**

PREP

20

COOK

20

SERVES

4

beer

crisp

juicy

margharita pizza

Often the simplest things in life are the best, as proven by this irresistibly moreish pizza.

1 Heat the oven to 230°C (450°F), Gas Mark 8.

2 Make the tomato sauce. Heat the oil in a large saucepan, add the onions and garlic and fry for 3 minutes. Add the tomatoes, vinegar, sugar and a dash of salt and pepper. Turn up the heat and simmer until the mixture has shrunk down by half to make a thick and rich tomato sauce.

3 Put the pizza bases on to baking sheets and brush with olive oil. Divide the tomato sauce among the pizzas and spread to within 5 mm (¼ inch) of the edge. Sprinkle over the cheese and olives and drizzle over a little more oil.

4 Place at the top of the oven and bake for about 20 minutes until bubbling and golden.

fancy tomato pizza

If you can't find all these different kinds of tomato, just use whatever you can buy. Peppers also work really well on this pizza.

1 Heat the oven to 230°C (450°F), Gas Mark 8.

2 Put the pizza bases on to baking sheets and brush with olive oil.

3 Dry the tomato slices on kitchen paper. Arrange all the tomatoes, basil, lemon rind and olives over the pizzas. Sprinkle with salt and pepper and drizzle over a little olive oil.

4 Place at the top of the oven and bake for 20 minutes, until the bases are crisp and the tops golden. Cut into slices and tuck in.

PREP

10

COOK

20

SERVES
4

star

mates

party

2 ready-to-cook **pizza bases**

olive oil, for brushing and drizzling

Topping:

1 large **plum tomato**, sliced

125 g (4 oz) **red cherry tomatoes**, halved

125 g (4 oz) **yellow pear tomatoes**, halved

4 **sun-dried tomatoes** in oil, drained and roughly chopped

handful of **basil** leaves, roughly chopped

2 teaspoons grated **lemon rind**

12 **black olives**, pitted

salt and **pepper**

280 g (9 oz) packet **pizza base mix**

1 tablespoon **olive oil**

1 **garlic clove**, crushed

2 **rosemary** sprigs, leaves removed and chopped

200 g (7 oz) frozen **spinach**, thawed

125 g (4 oz) **dolcelatte cheese**

4 tablespoons **mascarpone cheese**

pinch of grated **nutmeg**

150 g (5 oz) **mozzarella cheese**, sliced

25 g (1 oz) **Parmesan cheese**, grated

salt and **pepper**

PREP

20

COOK

12

SERVES

4

green

snack

hot

spinach and four cheese pizza

Pizza and beer are the ideal food for a Saturday night. So stock up on the lager and buy in the ingredients to make these luscious pizzas.

1 Heat the oven to 220°C (425°F), Gas Mark 7.

2 Make up the pizza dough with the olive oil according to the packet instructions, adding the garlic and rosemary to the mix. Divide the dough in half. Roll out each piece to a 35 cm (14 inch) round and put them on 2 baking sheets.

3 Squeeze out all the excess liquid from the spinach, put it in a bowl and mix in the dolcelatte and mascarpone. Mix in the grated nutmeg and some salt and pepper.

4 Put half the spinach mixture, half the mozzarella and half the Parmesan on top of one pizza base then sprinkle with pepper. Repeat to make the second pizza.

5 Bake for 12 minutes until bubbling, then cut in half and serve straight away.

speedy mediterranean pasta

This is one of those great sauces that you can easily adapt when you want to try something new. So chuck in some canned beans, pitted olives or walnuts – whatever you like really!

1 Put all the ingredients, except the pasta, in a saucepan and bring to the boil. Simmer, uncovered, for 15 minutes.

2 Cook the pasta according to the packet instructions until it is just tender then drain.

3 Pour the sauce into a blender or food processor and blend until smooth.

4 Toss the pasta with the sauce and dish up straight away. Delicious sprinkled with Parmesan and served with a green salad and French bread.

PREP

10

COOK

15

SERVES
4

saucy

fills

telly

400 g (13 oz) can chopped **tomatoes**

1 **onion**, chopped

1 **garlic clove**, crushed

2 tablespoons chopped **basil**

1 teaspoon dried **rosemary**

1 glass of **red wine**

375 g (12 oz) **pasta**

1 **red pepper**, cored, deseeded and cut into large squares

1 **courgette**, sliced

1 **red onion**, sliced

1 small **aubergine**, thinly sliced

8 **asparagus** spears, trimmed

5 tablespoons **olive oil**

375 g (12 oz) **linguine**

3 tablespoons frozen **peas**

125 g (4 oz) **Parmesan cheese**, grated

handful of **basil** leaves, roughly chopped

salt and **pepper**

PREP

10

COOK

25

SERVES

4

feast

smart

fresh

linguine with vegetables

A delicious dish packed with goodness – what more could you want?

1 Grill all the vegetables except for the peas under a hot grill for 10–15 minutes, turning them regularly so they brown but do not burn. Leave to cool slightly.

2 Peel the skin off the pepper and slice the flesh into strips. Tip into a dish with the courgette, onion, aubergine and asparagus, drizzle with olive oil and keep warm.

3 Cook the pasta according to the packet instructions, adding the peas for the last minute.

4 Drain the pasta and peas then pop back in the saucepan. Add the warm vegetables, sprinkle with salt and pepper and add the Parmesan. Toss well, adding a little more olive oil if it needs it. Finally, add the basil leaves, toss again and serve straight away.

goats' cheese linguine with herb butter

This is a very quick and simple sauce to make, but it tastes so good that your mates won't believe it took less than half-an-hour from start to finish.

1 Thickly slice the goats' cheese then cook under a hot grill for about 2 minutes until golden. Keep warm.

2 Melt the butter in a frying pan with the oil. Add the shallots and garlic and fry gently for 3 minutes. Stir in the herbs, capers and lemon juice and sprinkle with salt and pepper.

3 Cook the pasta according to the packet instructions. Drain and return to the saucepan. Add the goats' cheese and herby butter and toss together gently. Bellissimo!

PREP

5

COOK

20

SERVES

4

tasty

gooey

yum!

300 g (10 oz) **goats' cheese**

75 g (3 oz) **butter**

2 tablespoons **olive oil**

3 **shallots**, finely chopped

2 **garlic cloves**, crushed

25 g (1 oz) mixed **herbs** (such as tarragon, chervil, parsley or dill), chopped

3 tablespoons **capers**

juice of 1 **lemon**

375 g (12 oz) **linguine**

salt and **pepper**

275 g (9 oz) **spaghetti**

1 **onion**, chopped

50 g (2 oz) **butter**

250 g (8 oz) **spinach**, chopped

150 ml (¼ pint) **natural yogurt**

125 g (4 oz) **soft cheese**

1 teaspoon **lemon juice**

¼ teaspoon grated **nutmeg**

salt and **pepper**

spaghetti with creamy spinach

This fuss-free pasta has a decadently rich and creamy sauce. All you need is garlic bread and a glass of wine for a perfect meal ...

1 Cook the spaghetti according to the packet instructions and drain well.

2 Meanwhile, fry the onion in the butter in a large frying pan until soft but not browned. Add the spinach and fry for 2–3 minutes. Stir in the yogurt, cheese, lemon juice, nutmeg and salt and pepper and stir over a low heat without boiling.

3 Toss the pasta with the hot spinach sauce then dish up straight away.

pepper and brie penne

If you don't like Brie, then why not try this with Gorgonzola instead? Just swap the cheeses and use parsley instead of dill.

1 Grill the courgettes and peppers under a hot grill for 5–10 minutes, turning occasionally.

2 Cook the pasta according to the packet instructions. Drain well and return to the pan.

3 Add the grilled vegetables, Brie, oil and dill to the pasta. Sprinkle with salt and pepper, stir over a low heat for 5 minutes then dish up.

PREP

10

COOK

25

SERVES

4

fab!

best

moist

4 **courgettes**, sliced

1 **red pepper**, cored, deseeded and sliced

1 **green pepper**, cored, deseeded and sliced

1 **yellow pepper**, cored, deseeded and sliced

375g (12 oz) **penne**

175 g (6 oz) ripe **Brie**, cut into cubes

2 tablespoons **olive oil**

1 bunch of **dill**, chopped

salt and **pepper**

Ingredients

8 tablespoons **olive oil**

2 **aubergines**, cut into cubes

2 **red onions**, sliced

75 g (3 oz) **pine nuts**

3 **garlic cloves**, crushed

5 tablespoons **sun-dried tomato purée**

150 ml (¼ pint) **vegetable stock**

375 g (12 oz) **pasta**

100 g (3½ oz) **black olives**, pitted

salt and **pepper**

PREP

10

COOK

15

SERVES
4

green

super

feast

pasta with aubergines and pine nuts

Try cooking a flavoured pasta to go with the sauce, such as tomato and mushroom or spinach.

1 Heat the oil in a large frying pan and fry the aubergines and onions for 8–10 minutes until golden. Add the pine nuts and garlic and fry for 2 minutes. Stir in the sun-dried tomato purée and stock and cook for 2 minutes.

2 Meanwhile, cook the pasta according to the packet instructions.

3 Drain the pasta and tip back into the saucepan. Add the sauce, olives, salt and pepper and toss until combined. Serve at once.

penne with vodka, tomato and cream

The vodka gives this creamy sauce a distinctive kick – a real winner.

PREP

5

COOK

15

SERVES

6

tangy

posh

boozy

1 Cook the pasta according to the packet instructions.

2 Meanwhile, melt the butter in a saucepan over a low heat and stir in the tomato purée and cream. Take the pan off the heat and add the vodka and a little salt and pepper.

3 Drain the pasta, tip it back into the saucepan, pour over the sauce and mix well. Dish up, sprinkle with the basil and Parmesan and enjoy.

500 g (1 lb) **penne**

50 g (2 oz) **butter**

6 tablespoons **tomato purée**

450 ml (¾ pint) **single cream**

9 tablespoons **vodka**

1 tablespoon chopped **basil**

6 tablespoons grated **Parmesan cheese**

salt and **pepper**

75 g (3 oz) **Puy lentils**, rinsed

1 tablespoon **olive oil**

1 **onion**, finely chopped

1 **garlic clove**, crushed

2 small **carrots**, cut into cubes

2 small **courgettes**, cut into cubes

50 g (2 oz) **button mushrooms**, sliced

400 g (13 oz) can chopped **tomatoes**

150 ml (¼ pint) **vegetable stock**

2 tablespoons **tomato purée**

1 teaspoon dried **marjoram**

200 g (7 oz) **fusilli**

salt and **pepper**

lentil bolognese

This is an ideal meal to share with non-vegetarian friends. It can also be frozen for an instant homemade ready-meal when you've had a busy day.

good

cheap

tasty

1 Put the lentils into a saucepan, add plenty of cold water to cover and bring to the boil. Turn down the heat and simmer, uncovered, for 30 minutes or until tender. Drain and tip back into the pan.

2 Heat the oil in a saucepan, add the onion, garlic and carrots and fry for 4–5 minutes, stirring occasionally, until lightly browned. Add the courgettes and mushrooms and cook for 2 minutes. Stir in the tomatoes, stock, tomato purée, marjoram and a dash of salt and pepper.

3 Bring to the boil, cover and simmer for 5 minutes, stirring occasionally. Stir in the drained lentils, turn off the heat and cover.

4 Cook the pasta according to the packet instructions. Drain, tip back into the pan and toss with the sauce. Spoon into bowls and sprinkle with a little cheese if you like it.

penne with broad beans and feta cheese

This fantastic, herby pasta dish is packed with different tastes. Perfect with a green salad and herby garlic bread.

PREP

15

COOK

15

SERVES

2

1 Cook the pasta according to the packet instructions and drain well.

2 Meanwhile, cook the broad beans in a separate saucepan of boiling water for 4–5 minutes or until just tender. Drain and plunge into cold water to cool. Peel away and chuck out the outer shells.

3 Whisk all the dressing ingredients together in a small bowl with a good dash of salt and pepper.

4 Place the beans in a dish and stir in the pasta, tomatoes and herbs. Toss the pasta with the dressing, sprinkle with black pepper and toss in the feta. Eat immediately.

great

mates

fab!

200 g (7 oz) **penne**

200 g (7 oz) **broad beans**

50 g (2 oz) **sun-dried tomatoes** in oil, drained and roughly chopped

handful of mixed **herbs** (such as parsley, tarragon, chervil or chives), roughly chopped

50 g (2 oz) **feta cheese**, roughly chopped

black pepper

Dressing:

2 tablespoons **olive oil**

1 tablespoon **sherry vinegar**

½ teaspoon **mustard**

500 g (1 lb) **tagliatelle**

3 tablespoons **olive oil**

2 **garlic cloves**, finely chopped

500 g (1 lb) **cherry tomatoes**, halved

1 tablespoon **balsamic vinegar**

175 g (6 oz) **rocket**

4 tablespoons **Parmesan cheese** shavings

salt and **pepper**

PREP

10

COOK

12

SERVES

4

fast

saucy

good

tagliatelle with cherry tomatoes

This irresistible pasta tastes so good that you will want to make it again and again.

1 Cook the pasta according to the packet instructions.

2 Meanwhile, heat the oil in a frying pan and fry the garlic for 1 minute until golden. Add the tomatoes and cook for another minute.

3 Sprinkle the tomatoes with the vinegar, leave it to evaporate, then stir in the rocket and cook until it is just wilted.

4 Drain the pasta, toss with the tomatoes and sprinkle with salt and pepper. Dish up and top with plenty of Parmesan.

summer pasta of courgettes and dill

As the name suggests, this is an ideal lunch for a hot summer's day.

1 Cook the tagliatelle according to the packet instructions then drain well.

2 Meanwhile, heat the oil, add the garlic and fry for 1–2 minutes until lightly golden. Take the pan off the heat.

3 Stir the garlic and oil, courgettes and dill into the pasta. Add the lemon juice, sprinkle with salt and pepper and top with plenty of Parmesan cheese. Too good to be true!

PREP

COOK

SERVES

fresh

super

yum!

500 g (1 lb) **tagliatelle**

8 tablespoons **olive oil**

4 **garlic cloves**, sliced

4 **courgettes**, coarsely grated

4 tablespoons chopped **dill**

dash of **lemon juice**

4 tablespoons grated **Parmesan cheese**

salt and **pepper**

300g (10 oz) **fettuccine**

3 **red peppers**, cored, deseeded and halved

250 g (8 oz) **broccoli** florets

3 tablespoons **olive oil**

2 tablespoons **balsamic vinegar**

salt and **pepper**

PREP

10

COOK

15

SERVES

4

pals

easy

green

broccoli and red pepper fettuccine

Pasta is a real student favourite – cheap and easy, you just need to make sure that you don't overcook it or it will go soggy.

1 Cook the pasta according to the packet instructions. Drain, rinse under cold water, then drain again. Tip the pasta into a large bowl.

2 Grill the peppers under a hot grill, skin side up, until the skins have blackened and blistered. Leave to cool for 5 minutes.

3 Meanwhile, bring a large saucepan of water to the boil and boil the broccoli for 3 minutes. Drain, rinse under cold water and drain again.

4 Peel the peppers and slice the flesh into strips. Add to the pasta with the broccoli, olive oil and balsamic vinegar. Sprinkle with salt and pepper and toss well. Serve at once.

stripy macaroni cheese

If you can't be bothered to layer the vegetables, simply toss them all into the sauce with the pasta. You can also vary this dish by using 100 g (3½ oz) of thawed frozen spinach instead of the broccoli.

1 Cook the pasta according to the packet instructions.

2 Meanwhile, cook the broccoli, carrot and sweetcorn in boiling water until cooked but still crunchy.

3 Melt the butter in a saucepan. Stir in the flour and cook for 1 minute, then gradually mix in the milk and bring to the boil, stirring until the sauce is thick and smooth. Stir in the mustard and 75 g (3 oz) of the cheese.

4 Drain the macaroni and stir into the sauce. Spoon two-thirds of the macaroni cheese into a medium-sized ovenproof dish (if you use a glass dish you will be able to see the layers). Arrange the carrot, broccoli and sweetcorn in layers on top, then cover with the rest of the macaroni cheese.

5 Sprinkle with the rest of the cheese and breadcrumbs and pop under a hot grill for 5 minutes until golden brown.

PREP

10

COOK

15

SERVES

2

cheap

saucy

beer

125 g (4 oz) **macaroni**

100 g (3½ oz) **broccoli** florets

1 **carrot**, sliced

50 g (2 oz) frozen **sweetcorn**

15 g (½ oz) **butter**

15 g (½ oz) **plain flour**

200 ml (7 fl oz) **milk**

1 teaspoon **mustard**

100 g (3½ oz) **Cheddar cheese**, grated

1 tablespoon **breadcrumbs**

4 tablespoons **olive oil**

1 large **aubergine**, cut into cubes

1 **onion**, chopped

2 **red peppers**, cored, deseeded and cut into cubes

1 teaspoon dried **oregano**

175 g (6 oz) **penne**

1 quantity **Fresh Tomato Sauce** (see page 108)

2 **egg yolks**

250 g (8 oz) **crème fraîche** or **fromage frais**

2 tablespoons **milk**

125 g (4 oz) **feta cheese**, cut into cubes

salt and **pepper**

PREP

COOK

SERVES

yum!

fills

telly

aubergine and pepper pasta bake

This is comfort food at its best. Hearty, warming and filling, it's the perfect dish to concoct on a cold winter's day.

1 Heat half the oil in a large frying pan, add the aubergine and fry over a medium heat for 6–8 minutes until golden and tender. Remove from the pan and drain on kitchen paper. Add the rest of the oil and fry the onion, peppers and oregano for 10 minutes.

2 Heat the oven to 180°C (350°F), Gas Mark 4.

3 Cook the pasta according to the packet instructions. Drain well and immediately toss with the tomato sauce and fried vegetables. Add a good dash of salt and pepper then pour into a deep ovenproof dish.

4 Beat together the rest of the ingredients until evenly mixed then pour over the pasta mixture so it is covered. Bake for 35–40 minutes until the topping is set and golden. Great with a mixed salad.

vegetable lasagne

Lasagne is such a classic and straightforward but delicious dish to produce that everyone should know how to make it.

PREP

10

COOK

75

SERVES
4

feast

best

smart

2 tablespoons **vegetable oil**

150 g (5 oz) **green beans**, chopped

1 **onion**, thinly sliced

400 g (13 oz) can **tomatoes**

125 g (4 oz) **lentils**, rinsed

300 ml (½ pint) **water**

pinch of **oregano**

500 g (1 lb) **cream cheese**

2 **eggs**, beaten

125 g (4 oz) ready-cooked **lasagne** sheets

2 tablespoons grated **Parmesan cheese**

salt and **pepper**

1 Heat the oil in a saucepan and fry the beans and onion for 5 minutes. Sprinkle with salt and pepper then add the tomatoes, lentils, water and oregano and bring to the boil. Simmer for about 30 minutes, or until the lentils are tender.

2 Heat the oven to 180°C (350°F), Gas Mark 4.

3 Mix together the cream cheese and the beaten eggs.

4 Spread half the vegetable mixture over the bottom of a large ovenproof dish and cover with a third of the lasagne sheets. Pour over half the cheese mixture, then cover with another layer of lasagne sheets. Make a layer with the remaining vegetable mixture, cover with the remaining lasagne sheets and, finally, with the rest of the cheese mixture.

5 Sprinkle over the Parmesan and bake in the oven for 40 minutes.

125 g (4 oz) mini **macaroni**

4 **red peppers**, cored, deseeded and halved

2 large **tomatoes**, chopped

125 g (4 oz) **Cheddar cheese**, grated

2 **spring onions**, finely chopped

2 tablespoons chopped **parsley**

3 tablespoons **olive oil**

salt and **pepper**

PREP

COOK

SERVES

pasta-packed red peppers

Green peppers or yellow peppers work just as well here, and you can always use other kinds of mini pasta if you prefer. Just experiment with what you have in your store cupboard!

1 Heat the oven to 180°C (350°F), Gas Mark 4.

2 Cook the pasta according to the packet instructions then drain well.

3 Place the peppers on a baking sheet with the skins facing down.

4 Mix the macaroni, tomatoes, cheese, spring onions and parsley in a bowl. Spoon the mixture into the peppers, glug over the olive oil and sprinkle with salt and pepper.

5 Bake in the oven for 35–45 minutes until the filling is golden and bubbling. Delicious with crusty bread.

stuffed mushrooms

PREP

10

COOK

30

SERVES

4

Life isn't too short to stuff a mushroom if it tastes this good! In fact, this meal takes only 10 minutes to prepare and it's easy to make. Ideal when you need something at short notice.

1 Cook the pasta according to the packet instructions, then drain well.

2 Meanwhile, chop the mushroom stalks finely and put them on one side. Cook the mushroom caps for 5 minutes under a medium grill until just soft.

3 Put the onion into a large bowl. Add the chopped mushroom stalks, macaroni, walnuts, parsley, cheese and tomato purée. Mix well, add a dash of salt and pepper and then add enough of the beaten egg to stick everything together.

4 Divide the filling among the mushrooms, mounding the mixture up with a spoon. Drizzle over a little olive oil then grill for 15–20 minutes until the top of the stuffing is crisp and has started to brown. Delicious with a crisp mixed salad.

yum!

juicy

tasty

50 g (2 oz) mini **macaroni**

4 large **field mushrooms**

1 small **onion**, very finely chopped

25 g (1 oz) **walnuts**, chopped

1 tablespoon chopped **parsley**

25 g (1 oz) **Cheddar cheese**, cut into cubes

1 tablespoon **tomato purée**

1 **egg**, beaten

1 tablespoon **olive oil**

salt and **pepper**

1 kg (2 lb) floury **potatoes**

1–2 teaspoons **salt**

pinch of grated **nutmeg**

200 g (7 oz) **self-raising flour**

1 **egg**, beaten

plain flour, for dusting

3 tablespoons **pesto**

15 g (¼ oz) **butter**, melted

8 tablespoons grated **Parmesan cheese**

black pepper

45*

60

8

beer

hot

fills

potato gnocchi with pesto sauce

Gnocchi are light, airy little dumplings. To make great gnocchi you need to use floury potatoes, such as King Edward or Maris Piper, and handle the dough with a light touch.

1 Heat the oven to 200°C (400°F), Gas Mark 6. Bake the potatoes in the oven for 1 hour until tender. Leave to cool slightly.

2 Peel the cooked potatoes and mash while still warm. Add the salt and nutmeg and a dash of pepper. Add the flour and beaten egg and mix together as lightly as possible to form a soft dough. Do not overmix or the gnocchi will be tough and heavy.

3 Divide the dough into 4 balls. Dust your hands and work surface with flour and roll each ball into a sausage 2 cm (¾ inch) in diameter, then cut it into 1 cm (½ inch) pieces. Cover and chill for 30 minutes.

4 Press each gnocchi against the prongs of a fork to make a ridged pattern. Bring a saucepan of water to the boil. In three batches, simmer the gnocchi until they float, then cook for a further 20–30 seconds.

5 Lift the gnocchi out of the water and drain. Stir in the pesto and butter, sprinkle with Parmesan and pepper and tuck in.

* + chilling

bean soup with scones

tasty

best

share

This superb soup is served with tiny savoury scones. If you prefer, use small pasta shapes instead of the beans.

1 Heat the oil in a saucepan, add the onion and fry for 4–5 minutes until lightly browned. Stir in the carrot, celery and garlic and fry for 2 minutes, then add the beans, stock, tomato purée and a little salt and pepper. Bring to the boil and simmer for 20 minutes.

2 Heat the oven to 200°C (400°F), Gas Mark 6.

3 Meanwhile, make the scones. Put the flour into a bowl, add the butter and rub in with your fingertips until the mixture looks like breadcrumbs. Stir in the ground almonds, then the cheese. Add half of the egg and mix in enough milk to make a smooth, soft dough.

4 Lightly knead the dough, then roll out to 1.5 cm (¾ inch) thick. Cut into circles 5 cm (2 inch) across and place on a baking sheet. Brush the tops with beaten egg, then bake in the oven for 10–12 minutes until well risen.

5 Add the green beans and peas to the soup and simmer for 5 minutes.

6 Pour into bowls. Serve with warm buttered scones.

1 tablespoon **olive oil**

1 small **onion**, chopped

1 **carrot**, cut into cubes

2 **celery sticks**, sliced

1 **garlic clove**, crushed

100 g (3½ oz) cooked or drained canned **cannellini beans**

750 ml (1¼ pints) **vegetable stock**

2 teaspoons **tomato purée**

salt and **pepper**

Scones:

200 g (7 oz) **self-raising flour**

50 g (2 oz) **butter**, cubed

50 g (2 oz) **ground almonds**

125 g (4 oz) **Cheddar cheese**, grated

1 **egg**, beaten

150 ml (¼ pint) **milk**

To finish:

75 g (3 oz) **green beans**, sliced

3 tablespoons frozen **peas**

1 kg (2 lb) **tomatoes**, skinned

6 tablespoons **olive oil**

2 **onions**, chopped

4 **celery sticks**, sliced

4 **garlic cloves**, thinly sliced

175 g (6 oz) **mushrooms**, sliced

3 tablespoons **sun-dried tomato purée**

600 ml (1 pint) **vegetable stock**

1 tablespoon **sugar**

3 tablespoons **capers**

2 tablespoons chopped **basil**

salt and **pepper**

PREP

10

COOK

15

SERVES

4

yum!

great

easy

basil and tomato stew

Try to find really ripe, juicy and flavoursome tomatoes. If you can't, then add a bit of extra tomato purée.

1 Quarter and deseed the tomatoes, scooping out the pulp into a sieve over a bowl to catch the juices.

2 Heat 4 tablespoons of the oil in a large saucepan and fry the onions and celery for 5 minutes. Add the garlic and mushrooms and fry for another 3 minutes.

3 Add the tomatoes and their juices, sun-dried tomato purée, stock, sugar and capers and bring to the boil. Turn down the heat and simmer gently, uncovered, for 5 minutes.

4 Add the basil and a little salt and pepper and cook for 1 minute. Ladle into bowls, drizzle with the rest of the oil and serve with warm bread or toast.

caponata

Unlike most salads, caponata actually improves if it's left to stand for a little while.

1 Heat the oil in a large frying pan, add the aubergines and fry until golden and soft. Remove from the pan and drain on kitchen paper.

2 Add the onion and celery to the frying pan and fry for 6 minutes until they are soft but not brown.

3 Add the tomatoes and cook for 3 minutes, then add the vinegar, sugar, capers, olives, parsley and some salt and pepper. Simmer for 5 minutes then take off the heat and add the aubergines. Mix well, leave to cool then tuck in.

PREP

10

COOK

20

SERVES

4

pals

tasty

cool

6 tablespoons **olive oil**

2 **aubergines**, cut into cubes

1 **red onion**, chopped

3 **celery sticks**, chopped

5 **tomatoes**, skinned and roughly chopped

3 tablespoons **red wine vinegar**

1 tablespoon **sugar**

1 tablespoon **capers**

50 g (2 oz) **black olives**, pitted

handful of **parsley**, chopped

salt and **pepper**

2 tablespoons **olive oil**

50 g (2 oz) **butter**

2 **onions**, chopped

2 **garlic cloves**, crushed and chopped

500 g (1 lb) **mushrooms**, sliced

4 tablespoons **double cream**

4 tablespoons **white wine**

1 teaspoon chopped **thyme**

8 ready-cooked **lasagne sheets**

2 **red peppers**, cored, deseeded, skinned and thickly sliced

125 g (4 oz) **baby spinach** leaves

125 g (4 oz) **mozzarella cheese**, cut into 4 slices

50 g (2 oz) **Parmesan cheese**

salt and **pepper**

PREP

COOK

SERVES

fancy

mates

sexy

mozzarella stacks

This classy lasagne with a difference is a dish to impress with! Lusciously rich and tasty, it's always a winner.

1 Heat the oil and butter in a saucepan, add the onions and fry for 3 minutes. Add the garlic and cook for another minute. Add the mushrooms, turn up the heat and cook for 5 minutes.

2 Add the cream, white wine, thyme, salt and pepper and simmer for 4 minutes.

3 Put 4 sheets of lasagne in a large oven-proof dish. Dollop a generous spoonful of mushroom mixture onto each piece of lasagne, add some red pepper slices and half of the spinach leaves and put another piece of lasagne on top. Then add the rest of the spinach leaves, a slice of mozzarella, and top with a little more mushroom mixture. Finish with some Parmesan shavings.

4 Place the lasagne under a very hot grill and cook for 5 minutes until the mushroom mixture is bubbling and the Parmesan is golden. Yum!

melanzane parmigiana

A classic in Italian trattorias, this baked aubergine and cheese dish is always a treat.

PREP

40*

COOK

50

SERVES

6

beer

saucy

hot!

6 **aubergines**

2 tablespoons **olive oil**

1 quantity **Fresh Tomato Sauce** (see page 108)

250 g (8 oz) **Cheddar cheese,** grated

50 g (2 oz) **Parmesan cheese,** grated

salt

1 Cut the ends off the aubergines and cut them lengthways into thick slices. Sprinkle generously with salt and put to one side for about 10 minutes. Wash well, drain and pat dry on kitchen paper.

2 Heat the oven to 200°C (400°F), Gas Mark 6.

3 Brush the aubergine slices with oil and place them on 2 large baking sheets. Roast the aubergines in the oven for 10 minutes on each side until golden and tender.

4 Meanwhile, heat the tomato sauce and keep warm.

5 Spoon a little of the tomato sauce into an ovenproof dish and top with a layer of aubergine and some of the Cheddar. Continue with the layers, finishing with the Cheddar. Sprinkle over the Parmesan and bake for 30 minutes until bubbling and golden. Serve with a crisp green salad and bread to mop up the juices.

* + standing

125 g (4 oz) **butter**

1 tablespoon **olive oil**

1 **garlic clove**, crushed and chopped

1 **onion**, finely chopped

300 g (10 oz) **risotto rice**

1 litre (1¾ pints) hot **vegetable stock**

125 g (4 oz) **green beans**, topped and tailed and cut into 2.5 cm (1 inch) pieces

125 g (4 oz) frozen **peas**

125 g (4 oz) frozen **broad beans**

125 g (4 oz) **asparagus**, topped and tailed and cut into 2.5 cm (1 inch) pieces

125 g (4 oz) **baby spinach**, chopped

75 ml (3 fl oz) **white wine**

2 tablespoons chopped **parsley**

125 g (4 oz) **Parmesan cheese**, grated

salt and **pepper**

PREP

10

COOK

35

SERVES

4

share

fab!

juicy

green vegetable risotto

Quick and easy to cook, this is the perfect choice if you are making risotto for the first time.

1 Melt half the butter with the oil in a large saucepan. Add the garlic and onion and fry gently for 5 minutes but do not allow to brown.

2 Add the rice and stir well to coat the grains with the butter and oil. Add the hot stock, a large spoonful at a time, stirring each time until the stock is absorbed into the rice. Continue adding stock in this way, cooking until the rice is creamy but the grains are still firm. This should take about 20 minutes.

3 When you add the last of the stock, add the vegetables and wine, mix well and cook for 5 minutes.

4 Take the pan off the heat, sprinkle with salt and pepper and add the rest of the butter, the parsley and Parmesan. Mix well, then cover and leave to rest for a few minutes before dishing up this classic Italian dish.

lemon and leek risotto

50 g (2 oz) **butter**

1 **onion**, finely chopped

2 **garlic cloves**, crushed

2 **leeks**, trimmed, washed and sliced

250 g (8 oz) **risotto rice**

6 **bay leaves**

150 ml (¼ pint) **white wine**

1 litre (1¾ pints) hot **vegetable stock**

juice and rind of 1 large **lemon**

50 g (2 oz) **mascarpone cheese**

50 g (2 oz) **Parmesan cheese**, grated, plus extra for topping

salt and **pepper**

Adding the bay leaf to this lemon risotto isn't authentically Italian, but it does give it a lovely flavour.

1 Melt the butter in a large saucepan and fry the onion, garlic and leeks for 10 minutes until they are soft but not brown. Stir in the rice and bay leaves, and cook until the grains are glossy. Add the wine and simmer until the amount is reduced by half.

2 Add the hot stock, a large spoonful at a time, stirring each time until the stock is absorbed into the rice. Continue adding stock in this way, cooking until the rice is creamy but the grains are still firm. This should take about 20 minutes.

3 Add the lemon juice and rind and some salt and pepper and stir for 5 minutes. Add the mascarpone and Parmesan, stir once, then take off the heat, cover and leave to rest for a few minutes. Top with extra Parmesan if you want.

sexy

green

super

125 g (4 oz) **butter**

1 large **onion**, finely chopped

1–2 **red chillies**, deseeded and finely chopped

500 g (1 lb) **pumpkin**, peeled and roughly chopped

500 g (1 lb) **risotto rice**

1.5 litres (2½ pints) hot **vegetable stock**

3 tablespoons chopped **sage**

75 g (3 oz) **Parmesan cheese**, grated

salt and **pepper**

PREP

20

COOK

30

SERVES

4

tangy

moist

star

pumpkin, sage and chilli risotto

The chilli adds a real zing to this tasty risotto, and if you like your food spicy then chuck in a couple more.

1 Heat half the butter and fry the onion for 5 minutes until soft but not brown. Stir in the chillies and cook for 1 minute. Add the pumpkin and cook, stirring constantly, for 5 minutes.

2 Add the rice and stir well to coat the grains with the butter and oil. Add the hot stock, a large spoonful at a time, stirring each time until the stock is absorbed into the rice. Continue adding stock in this way, cooking until the rice is creamy but the grains are still firm. This should take about 20 minutes.

3 Add some salt and pepper, then stir in the sage, the rest of the butter and the Parmesan. Cover and leave the risotto to rest for a few minutes then enjoy.

cashew nut and green pepper risotto

The crunchiness of the nuts work perfectly here – all you need to complete the meal is a bottle of good red wine.

PREP

5

COOK

50

SERVES

5

1 Heat the oil in a large frying pan, add the onion and pepper and fry gently for about 5 minutes until soft. Add the sweetcorn and rice and cook, stirring, for 1 minute.

2 Stir in the stock and bring to the boil. Turn down the heat and simmer, uncovered, for 30–40 minutes until the rice is tender.

3 Stir in the soy sauce and cashew nuts and cook for a further 5–10 minutes until all the stock is absorbed.

best

feast

yum!

2 teaspoons **vegetable oil**

1 **onion**, finely sliced

1 **green pepper**, cored, deseeded and finely sliced

125 g (4 oz) **sweetcorn kernals**

300 g (10 oz) **brown rice**

900 ml (1½ pints) hot **vegetable stock**

1 tablespoon **soy sauce**

125 g (4 oz) **cashew nuts**

orient express

vegetable oil, for deep-frying

250 g (8 oz) tofu, cut into cubes

2 tablespoons vegetable oil

1 garlic clove, sliced

250 g (8 oz) broccoli florets

125 g (4 oz) green beans, halved

2 carrots, thinly sliced

150 ml (¼ pint) hot vegetable stock

3 tablespoons soy sauce

2 tablespoons soft brown sugar

2 tablespoons sweet chilli sauce

125 g (4 oz) bean sprouts

2 tablespoons chopped mint

PREP

10

COOK

10

SERVES

4

light

feast

crisp

tofu with stir-fried vegetables

Tofu is an excellent source of protein, and it's a healthy staple in most vegetarian diets. For a heartier meal add some boiled or fried rice.

1 In a wok or large frying pan heat the oil and deep-fry the tofu for 2–3 minutes until it is crisp and golden. Drain on kitchen paper and keep warm.

2 Heat the vegetable oil in a wok or large frying pan and fry the garlic for 1 minute. Remove the garlic, but not the oil, and throw it away. Add the broccoli, beans to the oil and carrots and stir-fry for 3 minutes.

3 Mix the stock, soy sauce, sugar and chilli sauce together in a small bowl and add to the wok. Cook for 2–3 minutes until the vegetables are tender. Stir in the bean sprouts and mint and serve with the warm tofu.

spicy coconut milk noodles

A single Thai chilli gives this dish a really fiery kick. Use a mild chilli instead if you are feeling cautious.

1 Put the noodles into a large bowl and cover with boiling water. Leave to stand while you prepare the vegetables.

2 Heat the oil in a wok or large frying pan and gently fry the onion, chilli, garlic, ginger, coriander, turmeric and lemon grass for 5 minutes.

3 Drain the noodles. Pour the coconut milk and stock into the wok and bring just to the boil, then turn down the heat and stir in the cabbage, beans, mushrooms and noodles. Cover and simmer for 5 minutes then stir in the peanuts, salt and pepper and dish up.

PREP

15

COOK

15

SERVES

4

fast

green

spicy

125 g (4 oz) dried medium **egg noodles**

2 tablespoons **vegetable oil**

1 **onion**, chopped

1 **red chilli**, deseeded and sliced

3 **garlic cloves**, sliced

5 cm (2 inch) **root ginger**, peeled and grated

2 teaspoons ground **coriander**

½ teaspoon **turmeric**

1 **lemon grass** stalk, finely sliced

400 ml (14 fl oz) can **coconut milk**

300 ml (½ pint) **vegetable stock**

125 g (4 oz) **cabbage**, finely shredded

275 g (9 oz) **green beans**, sliced diagonally

150 g (5 oz) **mushrooms**, sliced

75 g (3 oz) unsalted, shelled **peanuts**

salt and **pepper**

250 g (8 oz) **Chinese leaves**, chopped into 2.5 cm (1 inch) pieces

50 g (2 oz) **cauliflower** florets

50 g (2 oz) **broccoli** (preferably Chinese)

50 g (2 oz) **white cabbage**, chopped

2 **baby corn cobs**, sliced diagonally

1 large **tomato**, cut into 8 pieces

5 **garlic cloves**, chopped

50 g (2 oz) unsalted **cashew nuts**

1½ tablespoons **soy sauce**

1 teaspoon **sugar**

100 ml (3½ fl oz) **water**

2½ tablespoons **vegetable oil**

black pepper

quick

easy

hot

stir-fried vegetables with cashews

Stir-fries are quick, cheap and easy, and they taste superb. So why not make them a regular part of your cooking repertoire?

1 Mix all the ingredients together, except for the oil and pepper, in a large bowl.

2 Heat the oil in a wok or large frying pan then throw in the contents of the bowl and cook over a high heat, stirring, for 2–3 minutes.

3 Sprinkle with black pepper and dish up immediately.

stir-fried green beans

Why not cook up a banquet for friends? With Fried Rice with Beans and Tofu (see page 146) and Sweet Potato and Spinach Curry (see page 159) this would make a real feast.

1 Heat the oil in a wok or large frying pan. Add the garlic, shallots and ginger and stir-fry over a medium heat for 1 minute. Stir in the chilli and salt and continue stir-frying for 30 seconds.

2 Add the green beans and cashew nuts to the wok and toss well to mix everything together. Stir-fry quickly for 1 minute.

3 Add the stock, wine, soy sauce, vinegar and sugar and bring to the boil. Turn down the heat slightly and stir-fry for about 4 minutes, stirring and turning until the beans are cooked and the liquid has thickened. Sprinkle with black pepper and dish up straight away.

PREP

10

COOK

10

SERVES

4

pals

best

fancy

3 tablespoons **vegetable oil**

2 **garlic cloves**, crushed

2 **shallots**, thinly sliced

1 slice **root ginger**, peeled and chopped

1 **red chilli**, deseeded and finely chopped

½ teaspoon **salt**

500 g (1 lb) **green beans**, trimmed and cut into 5 cm (2 inch) lengths

50 g (2 oz) unsalted **cashew nuts**

125 ml (4 fl oz) **vegetable stock**

2 tablespoons **white wine**

1 tablespoon **soy sauce**

1 teaspoon **vinegar**

1 teaspoon **sugar**

black pepper

50 g (2 oz) dried **shiitake mushrooms**

2 tablespoons **vegetable oil**

5 cm (2 inches) **root ginger,** peeled and chopped

2 **spring onions**, finely chopped

1 **garlic clove**, crushed

250 g (8 oz) **button mushrooms**, halved

200 g (7 oz) can **straw mushrooms**, drained

1 teaspoon **chilli powder**

2 teaspoons **dry sherry** (optional)

2 teaspoons **soy sauce**

2 tablespoons **vegetable stock**

pinch of **sugar**

pinch of **salt**

1 teaspoon **sesame oil**

PREP

5*

COOK

10

SERVES

4

tangy

posh

great

stir-fried mixed mushrooms

Mushrooms go really well with everything, and taste great with noodles, rice or stir-fried vegetables.

1 Soak the dried mushrooms in warm water for 30 minutes. Drain and squeeze them, then cut off and throw away the hard stalks. Thinly slice the mushrooms.

2 Heat the oil in a wok or large frying pan over a medium heat. Add the ginger, spring onions and the garlic and stir-fry for 10 seconds. Then add the shiitake mushrooms and button mushrooms and continue stir-frying for 5 minutes.

3 Add the straw mushrooms, chilli powder, sherry, soy sauce, stock, sugar, salt and sesame oil. Mix well and stir-fry for 5 minutes, then dish up immediately.

* + soaking

fragrant aubergine stir-fry

The crispiness of the aubergine chips and the sweetness of the tangy sauce in this dish make a great combination.

PREP

15

COOK

7

SERVES

2

juicy

fab!

super

1 Heat the oil in a wok or large frying pan. Add the aubergine 'chips' and deep-fry for 1–2 minutes until golden. Remove and drain on kitchen paper.

2 Carefully pour off the oil to leave only 1 tablespoonful in the wok. Quickly stir-fry the spring onions with the ginger and garlic, then mix in the soy sauce and chilli sauce. Add the aubergine chips and stir-fry for 1–2 minutes.

3 Mix the cornflour with a little water and then stir it into the mixture in the wok. Cook until the sauce thickens then tuck in.

vegetable oil, for deep-frying

250 g (8 oz) **aubergines**, peeled and cut into chip-sized strips

2 **spring onions**, finely chopped

1 slice **ginger root**, peeled and finely chopped

1 **garlic clove**, finely chopped

1 tablespoon **soy sauce**

2 teaspoons **sweet chilli sauce**

2 tablespoons **cornflour**

vegetable oil, for deep-frying

125 g (4 oz) tofu, cut into cubes

2 eggs

250 g (8 oz) cold cooked rice

3 teaspoons sugar

1½ tablespoons soy sauce

2 teaspoons crushed dried chillies

1 teaspoon salt

125 g (4 oz) green beans, finely chopped

fun

cheap

tasty

fried rice with beans and tofu

Fried rice is really easy to cook and you can add whatever vegetables you like to jazz it up. Sweetcorn, peas and peppers work particularly well.

1 Heat the oil in a wok or large frying pan and deep-fry the tofu over a moderate heat until golden. Remove and drain on kitchen paper. Pour the oil out of the wok, leaving about 2 tablespoonfuls. Heat this oil until hot, then crack the eggs into it, breaking the yolks and stirring them around.

2 Add the rice, sugar, soy sauce, chillies and salt and turn up the heat to high. Stir-fry vigorously for 1 minute.

3 Turn down the heat and add the green beans and tofu. Turn up the heat again and stir-fry vigorously for another minute, then dish up straight away.

green curry with straw mushrooms

Green curry is best served with rice or noodles as they will soak up the delightfully creamy sauce.

1 Heat the coconut milk in a saucepan with the curry paste. Stir well so it's all mixed in. Add the stock and then the aubergines, sugar, salt, soy sauce, ginger and mushrooms.

2 Bring to the boil and cook, stirring, for 2 minutes. Add the green pepper, turn down the heat and cook for 1 minute.

3 Serve in a bowl, drizzled with a little extra coconut milk.

PREP

COOK

SERVES

4

easy

fast

sexy

300 ml (½ pint) **coconut milk**

40 g (1⅛ oz) **green curry paste**

300 ml (⅙ pint) **vegetable stock**

4 small round **aubergines**, each cut into 8 pieces

40 g (1½ oz) **soft brown sugar**

1 teaspoon **salt**

4 teaspoons **soy sauce**

25 g (1 oz) **root ginger**, peeled and finely chopped

425 g (14 oz) can **straw mushrooms**, drained

50 g (2 oz) **green pepper**, thinly sliced

crispy tofu in tomato sauce

vegetable oil, for deep-frying

6 pieces of **tofu**, halved and cut into bite-size triangles

3 large **tomatoes**, skinned, deseeded and finely chopped

100 ml (3½ fl oz) **vegetable stock**

⅓ teaspoon **sugar**

salt

saucy

cool

beer

Tofu has a lovely crunchy texture and is fantastic fried. If you like your food spicy then just add a one or two finely chopped chillies to the tomato sauce.

1 Heat the oil in a wok or large frying pan. Add the tofu and stir-fry until it is golden brown. Remove from the oil and drain on kitchen paper.

2 Put the tomatoes in a saucepan with the stock, sugar and a dash of salt. Bring to the boil, then simmer gently for 15–20 minutes.

3 Add the tofu triangles and simmer for 10–15 minutes until the sauce is nice and thick. Eat straight away.

three-bean stir-fry

If you are feeling a bit run-down this will be the perfect pick-me-up.

PREP

15

COOK

20

SERVES

4

good

feast

pals

1 Heat the oil in a wok or large frying pan until it is hot. Add the onion and garlic and stir-fry over a gentle heat until the onion has softened.

2 Add the three types of beans and turn up the heat to high. Toss well to mix then add the tomatoes a little at a time, stir-frying until the tomatoes are mixed in with the beans.

3 Add the tomato purée and sugar, then boil until the liquid reduces, stirring constantly. Take off the heat, stir in the parsley and a dash of salt and pepper. Dish up straight away.

3 tablespoons **vegetable oil**

1 **red onion**, finely chopped

2 **garlic cloves**, crushed

425 g (14 oz) can **butter beans**, drained and rinsed

425 g (14 oz) can **red kidney beans**, drained and rinsed

425 g (14 oz) can **cannellini beans**, drained and rinsed

400 g (13 oz) can chopped **tomatoes**, drained

1 tablespoon **tomato purée**

1 teaspoon **sugar**

handful of chopped **parsley**

salt and **pepper**

1 bunch of **spring onions**, roughly chopped

5 cm (2 inches) **root ginger**, peeled and chopped

2 **lemon grass stalks**, roughly chopped

small handful of **coriander** leaves

3 **garlic cloves**, roughly chopped

1 tablespoon **sugar**

1 tablespoon **soy sauce**

75 g (3 oz) **breadcrumbs**

300 g (10 oz) **tofu**

1 **egg**

plain flour, for dusting

vegetable oil, for shallow-frying

salt and **pepper**

PREP

10

COOK

8

SERVES

4

tangy

snack

mates

lemon grass and tofu nuggets

Try making a sweet dipping sauce from honey, soy sauce, orange juice and red chilli to go with this.

1 In a blender or food processor blend the spring onions, ginger, lemon grass, coriander and garlic until chopped but still chunky. Add the sugar, soy sauce, breadcrumbs, tofu, egg, salt and pepper and blend until just mixed.

2 With lightly floured hands make spoonfuls of the mixture into flat cakes.

3 Heat the oil in a wok or large frying pan and gently fry half the tofu cakes for 1–2 minutes on each side until golden. Drain on kitchen paper and keep warm while you fry the rest. Dip into a spicy dip of your choice. Fantastic!

stir-fried vegetable omelette

Use whatever vegetables you like, such as mushrooms, sweetcorn, peas or cauliflower.

PREP

COOK

SERVES

2 tablespoons **vegetable oil**

1 **onion**, finely chopped

1 **garlic clove**, crushed

2 **potatoes**, quartered and finely sliced

½ **green** or **red pepper**, cored, deseeded and finely chopped

4–6 **broccoli** florets

3 **tomatoes**, sliced

¼ **cucumber**, chopped

5–6 large **eggs**, beaten

1 tablespoon chopped **parsley**

black pepper

1 Heat the oil in a wok or large frying pan and stir-fry the onion until soft. Add the garlic, potatoes, pepper and broccoli and stir-fry for 6 minutes until tender but still crisp. Add a little water if the vegetables start to stick to the pan.

2 Stir in the tomatoes and cucumber, then spread the mixture evenly around the base of the pan. Pour the eggs over the vegetables, stir well and flatten the mixture again. Cook, without stirring, until the eggs begin to set, then place the pan under a hot grill until the top of the omelette has set.

3 Cut the omelette into wedges, sprinkle with parsley and pepper and eat hot.

275 g (9 oz) **Camargue red rice**

600 ml (1 pint) hot **vegetable stock**

600 ml (1 pint) boiling **water**

3 tablespoons **olive oil**

1 large **red onion**, chopped

2 tablespoons **paprika**

3 **garlic cloves**, crushed

1 teaspoon **saffron** threads

2 **red peppers**, cored, deseeded and sliced

finely grated rind of 1 **lemon**

2 teaspoons **lemon juice**

4 **tomatoes**, roughly chopped

small handful of **parsley**, roughly chopped

50 g (2 oz) **black olives**, pitted

salt and **pepper**

PREP

5

COOK

25

SERVES

4

posh

sexy

share

red rice and pepper pilaf

Crack open the bubbly – this exotic dish is cause for a celebration. If you can't get hold of red rice then use brown rice instead.

1 Put the rice, stock and boiling water into a large saucepan. Bring to the boil, cover and simmer for 25 minutes, stirring frequently.

2 Meanwhile, heat the oil in a saucepan. Add the onion and fry for 3 minutes. Add the paprika, garlic, saffron and peppers and fry for 5 minutes.

3 Stir in the lemon rind and juice, tomatoes and parsley and cook gently, uncovered, for 5 minutes.

4 Drain the rice and add to the saucepan with the olives and a good dash of salt and pepper. Toss together until well mixed, then dish up.

lentil and rice pilaf

Sweet and spicy, this delicious pilaf has the distinctive flavours of eastern Mediterranean cooking. If you don't have pine nuts, you can use unsalted peanuts or cashew nuts instead.

1 Put the lentils in a saucepan, add just enough water to cover and bring to the boil. Boil rapidly for 10 minutes, then drain.

2 Meanwhile, fry the pine nuts in a large frying pan without any oil, shaking the pan frequently, until the nuts are lightly toasted. Tip them on to a plate.

3 Heat the olive oil in the frying pan, add the onion, garlic, allspice and ginger and fry for 3 minutes. Add the rice and cook for 1 minute. Add the stock and lentils and bring to a simmer. Cover and cook gently for 20 minutes until the rice and lentils are tender, adding a little more water if the mixture becomes dry.

4 Stir the dried fruit, parsley, pine nuts and a little salt and pepper into the rice and cook for 2 minutes. Lovely!

PREP

10

COOK

35

SERVES
4

tasty

super

fruity

125 g (4 oz) large **green** or **Puy lentils**

40 g (1½ oz) **pine nuts**

2 tablespoons **olive oil**

1 large **onion**, chopped

2 **garlic cloves**, sliced

¼ teaspoon ground **allspice**

4 cm (1½ inch) piece **root ginger**, peeled and chopped

125 g (4 oz) **long-grain** or **basmati rice**

300 ml (½ pint) **vegetable stock**

50 g (2 oz) ready-to-eat **dried apricots** or **prunes**, sliced

small handful of **parsley**, roughly chopped

salt and **pepper**

2 tablespoons **vegetable oil**

1 **onion**, sliced

1 teaspoon ground **coriander**

2 teaspoons ground **cumin**

2 **garlic cloves**, crushed

5 cm (2 inch) piece of **root ginger**, peeled and chopped

400 g (13 oz) can chopped **tomatoes**

150 ml (¼ pint) **water**

1 **green chilli**, deseeded and finely chopped

2 **potatoes**, cut into cubes

2 **carrots**, sliced

175 g (6 oz) **okra**, chopped

250 g (8 oz) **cauliflower** florets

2 tablespoons chopped **coriander**

salt and **pepper**

PREP

30

COOK

30

SERVES

4

booze

mates

telly

vegetable curry

All you need with this is some rice and warm naan bread, mango chutney and an ice-cold beer. Sport on the TV would be good too …

1 Heat the oil in a large saucepan, add the onion and fry until soft. Add the coriander, cumin, garlic and ginger and fry for 1 minute, stirring constantly. Add the tomatoes, water, chilli, potatoes, carrots, okra and cauliflower and a dash of salt and pepper.

2 Mix well then cover and cook gently for 20 minutes, until tender. Stir in the coriander then dish up on a mound of rice and with some warm naan bread.

simple vegetable biriyani

Don't taste this until the end – it takes time for the flavours to infuse, and the chilli will become hotter as it cooks. You can always add a little more curry powder at the end if you want.

1 Cook the rice in a saucepan of boiling water for 5 minutes. Drain, run under cold water, then drain again. Spread out the rice on a plate so it dries a little.

2 Heat 2 tablespoons of the oil in a frying pan, add half the onion and fry over a medium heat for 10 minutes until very crisp and golden. Remove and drain on kitchen paper.

3 Add the rest of the oil to the frying pan and fry the rest of the onion with the garlic and ginger for 5 minutes. Add the sweet potato, carrot, curry paste and spices and fry for another 10 minutes until light golden.

4 Add the stock and tomatoes, bring to the boil, cover and simmer for 20 minutes. Add the cauliflower and peas and cook for another 8–10 minutes until the vegetables are tender.

5 Mix in the rice and cashew nuts. Cook, stirring for 3 minutes, then cover and take off the heat. Leave for 5 minutes, then dish up, sprinkling on the crispy onions and topping with the hard-boiled eggs.

PREP

25

COOK

60

SERVES

4

fills

beer

smart

250 g (8 oz) **basmati rice**

6 tablespoons **vegetable oil**

2 large **onions**, sliced

2 **garlic cloves**, crushed

2 teaspoons grated **root ginger**

250 g (8 oz) **sweet potato**, cut into cubes

2 large **carrots**, cut into cubes

1 tablespoon **curry paste**

2 teaspoons **turmeric**

1 teaspoon ground **cinnamon**

1 teaspoon **chilli powder**

300 ml (½ pint) **vegetable stock**

4 **tomatoes**, skinned, deseeded and cubed

175 g (6 oz) **cauliflower** florets

125 g (4 oz) frozen **peas**, thawed

50 g (2 oz) **cashew nuts**

2 **hard-boiled eggs** (see page 20), cut into quarters

salt and **pepper**

2 tablespoons **vegetable oil**

1 **onion**, finely chopped

1 teaspoon grated **root ginger**

1 **green chilli**, deseeded and chopped

500 g (1 lb) **button mushrooms**, halved

1 teaspoon **chilli powder**

½ teaspoon **turmeric**

2 teaspoons ground **cumin**

1 tablespoon ground **coriander**

200 g (7 oz) can chopped **tomatoes**

1 teaspoon **sugar**

3 tablespoons **single cream**

2 tablespoons chopped **coriander** leaves

salt and **pepper**

PREP

10

COOK

20

SERVES

4

fancy

star

fresh

mushroom korma

This is the perfect choice for those who love aromatic rather than fiery dishes. It's best served with brown rice.

1 Heat the oil in a large saucepan and fry the onions until soft and lightly browned.

2 Add the ginger, chilli and mushrooms and fry for 5 minutes. Add the chilli powder, turmeric, cumin, coriander, tomatoes and sugar then cover and cook gently for 8–10 minutes.

3 Stir in the cream and coriander, sprinkle with salt and pepper and eat straight away.

mixed bean curry

Supremely good for you, this curry is packed with protein and tasty spices. Who says it's difficult eat healthy food?

PREP

25

COOK

30

SERVES

4

great

fab!

fills

1 Heat the butter in a saucepan and fry the onions for 10 minutes until golden brown. Add the garlic and fry for a few seconds only, then add the coriander, garam masala and chilli powder and fry for a few seconds. Stir in the tomatoes and sugar with a dash of salt and pepper then turn down the heat and cook for 10 minutes.

2 Add the beans, stir thoroughly, then cover and cook gently until heated through. Delicious with rice and poppadoms.

125 g (4 oz) **butter**

2 **onions**, finely chopped

3 **garlic cloves**, crushed

1 tablespoon ground **coriander**

1 teaspoon **garam masala**

1 teaspoon **chilli powder**

400 g (13 oz) can chopped **tomatoes**

1 teaspoon **sugar**

425 g (14 oz) can **butter beans**, drained and rinsed

425 g (14 oz) can **red kidney beans**, drained and rinsed

425 g (14 oz) can **cannellini beans**, drained and rinsed

salt and **pepper**

massaman potato curry

750 ml (1¼ pints) **coconut milk**

400 g (13 oz) **potatoes**, peeled and cut into even-sized pieces

50 g (2 oz) **roasted peanuts**, crushed

1 large **onion**, chopped

5 tablespoons **water**

75 g (3 oz) **brown sugar**

2 teaspoons **salt**

Massaman curry paste:

3 **cardamom** pods

1 teaspoon **coriander** seeds

1 teaspoon **cumin** seeds

2 **cloves**

6 small **red chillies**

2 **garlic cloves**, halved

1 teaspoon ground **cinnamon**

1 cm (½ inch) **root ginger**, peeled and chopped

3 **shallots**, chopped

1 **lemon grass** stalk, chopped

juice of ½ **lime**

COOK

25

SERVES

4

tasty

yum!

beer

Don't be daunted by the long list of ingredients – just take your time creating a masterpiece. If you have any curry paste left over you can keep it in a screw-top jar in the fridge for up to 3 weeks.

1 First make the curry paste. Remove the seeds from the cardamom pods and fry the seeds with the coriander and cumin seeds and the cloves in a frying pan without any oil for 2 minutes. Tip the fried spices into a blender or food processor and blend with the rest of the curry paste ingredients to make a thick paste.

2 Heat the coconut milk in a large saucepan and add 2 tablespoons of the curry paste. Mix well, then heat until simmering.

3 Turn down the heat, add the potatoes to the saucepan and cook for 6 minutes.

4 Add the peanuts, onion, water, sugar and salt. Stir well so the sugar dissolves and continue to simmer, stirring, for 5 minutes.

5 Turn up the heat and let the liquid bubble until the potato is tender. Gorgeous with naan bread or rice and a salad.

sweet potato and spinach curry

Everyone loves a good curry, and your mates are bound to love you even more when you serve up this extremely tasty dish.

PREP

15

COOK

25

SERVES

4

pals

boozy

saucy

1 Cook the sweet potato in a large saucepan of boiling water for 8–10 minutes, then drain and put to one side.

2 Heat the oil in a saucepan, add the onion, garlic and turmeric and fry over a gentle heat, stirring often, for 3 minutes. Stir in the chilli and fry for another 2 minutes.

3 Add the coconut milk, stir well, then simmer for 3–4 minutes until the coconut milk has thickened slightly. Stir in the cooked sweet potatoes and a dash of salt, then cook the curry for 4 minutes.

4 Stir in the spinach, cover the pan and simmer gently for 2–3 minutes, or until the spinach has wilted and the curry has heated through. Best eaten with naan bread or chapattis.

500 g (1 lb) **sweet potatoes**, peeled and cut into large chunks

3 tablespoons **vegetable oil**

1 **red onion**, chopped

2 **garlic cloves**, crushed

1 teaspoon **turmeric**

1 large **red chilli**, deseeded and chopped

400 ml (14 fl oz) **coconut milk**

250 g (8 oz) **baby spinach**, washed

salt

3 tablespoons **vegetable oil**

1 small **onion**, sliced

2 **garlic cloves**, chopped

2 teaspoons grated **root ginger**

1 teaspoon ground **coriander**

½ teaspoon ground **cumin**

½ teaspoon **turmeric**

¼ teaspoon ground **cinnamon**

500 g (1 lb) **pumpkin** flesh, cut into cubes

2 tablespoons hot **curry paste**

2 **tomatoes**, chopped

2 dried **red chillies**

300 ml (½ pint) **vegetable stock**

400 g (13 oz) can **chickpeas**, drained

1 large under-ripe **banana**, thickly sliced

1 tablespoon chopped **coriander**

COOK

50

SERVES

4

tangy

fancy

smart

pumpkin, chickpea and banana curry

This combination of flavours may sound rather unusual (or plain weird!), but the different tastes work together really well. Try it and you'll be converted!

1 Heat 2 tablespoons of the oil in a saucepan, add the onion, garlic, ginger and ground spices and fry over a medium heat for 5–6 minutes until the onion is lightly browned.

2 Put the pumpkin in a bowl, add the curry paste and toss well so the pumpkin is coated.

3 Add the tomatoes, chillies and stock to the onion mixture, bring to the boil and simmer gently for 15 minutes.

4 Meanwhile, heat the rest of the oil in a frying pan, add the pumpkin and fry for 5 minutes until golden.

5 Add the pumpkin to the tomato sauce with the chickpeas, cover and cook for 15 minutes until the pumpkin is tender.

6 Mix the banana into the curry and cook for 5 more minutes, then stir in the coriander. Dish up straight away with rice or naan bread.

mung dhal

This rich lentil purée is so versatile. It goes really well with vegetable stew, rice or naan bread, as well as making an excellent spread for sandwiches.

1 Put the lentils in a large saucepan with the turmeric, chilli powder, cinnamon and stock. Stir well, bring to the boil then turn down the heat immediately, cover and simmer for 20–40 minutes until the lentils are soft and the stock is almost absorbed. The mixture should be creamy, but the lentils should keep some of their texture.

2 Heat the oil in a frying pan and fry the onion and garlic until they are a light golden colour. Stir in the cumin seeds and fry until they begin to splutter. Pour over the lentil mixture and stir well. Stir in the coriander, sprinkle with salt and dish up.

great

basic

cool

250 g (8 oz) **split red lentils**, washed and drained

½ teaspoon **turmeric**

½ teaspoon **chilli powder**

2.5 cm (1 inch) piece of **cinnamon** stick

750 ml (1¼ pints) hot **vegetable stock**

2 tablespoons **vegetable oil**

1 large **onion**, thinly sliced

1–2 **garlic cloves**, crushed

½ teaspoon **cumin seeds**

1 tablespoon finely chopped **coriander**

salt

1 tablespoon **vegetable oil**

2 **garlic cloves**, finely chopped

1 teaspoon freshly grated **ginger**

1 teaspoon **cumin** seeds

1 teaspoon **coriander** seeds, roughly crushed

½ teaspoon dried **chilli** flakes

625 g (1¼ lb) cooked **beetroot**, cut into wedges

150 ml (¼ pint) **coconut milk**

¼ teaspoon ground **cardamom seeds**

grated rind and juice of 1 **lime**

handful of chopped **coriander**

salt and **pepper**

PREP

10

COOK

6

SERVES

4

party

tasty

juicy

spiced beetroot

Spiced with cardamom, coriander, cumin and lime, this dish will change the way you feel about the colourful – but humble – beetroot.

1 Heat the oil in a large frying pan and add the garlic, ginger, cumin, coriander seeds and chilli flakes. Fry for 1–2 minutes then add the beetroot. Fry, stirring gently, for 1 minute then add the coconut milk, cardamom, lime rind and juice. Cook over a medium heat for 2–3 minutes.

2 Stir in the coriander and a dash of salt and pepper. Delicious either hot or just warm.

curried sweetcorn patties

Crispy, crunchy patties with a creamy yogurt dip – perfect finger food!

fab!

share

snack

1 Keep 4 tablespoons of the sweetcorn on one side and put the rest in a blender or food processor with the cornflour, plain flour, egg, salt, curry powder, chilli powder and turmeric. Blend briefly until mixed, then tip into a bowl and stir in the shallot and coriander and the rest of the sweetcorn.

2 Make the yogurt dip by mixing together all the ingredients.

3 Heat the oil in a saucepan to deep-fry the patties (it is hot enough when a cube of bread browns within 30 seconds). Drop spoonfuls of the mixture into the oil and cook in batches for 3–4 minutes per batch until crisp and golden. Remove with a spoon and drain on kitchen paper.

4 Dip the hot patties into the lemony yogurt dip and enjoy.

375 g (12 oz) **sweetcorn**

2 tablespoons **cornflour**

2 tablespoons **plain flour**

1 **egg**, lightly beaten

¼ teaspoon **salt**

1 teaspoon **curry powder**

½ teaspoon **chilli powder**

¼ teaspoon **turmeric**

1 **shallot**, finely chopped

2 tablespoons chopped **coriander**

vegetable oil, for deep frying

Yogurt dip:

4 tablespoons **natural yogurt**

1 tablespoon **lemon juice**

1 tablespoon chopped **coriander**

1 teaspoon **clear honey**

¼ teaspoon **garam masala**

¼ teaspoon **salt**

mushroom and pea curry

PREP

10

COOK

20

SERVES

4

2 tablespoons **vegetable oil**

50 g (2 oz) **onion**, finely sliced

¼ teaspoon **cumin** seeds, crushed

¼ teaspoon **mustard** seeds

125 g (4 oz) **tomatoes**, chopped

1 **green chilli**, deseeded and finely chopped

425 g (14 oz) **button mushrooms**, halved (quartered if large)

150 g (5 oz) frozen **peas**

½ teaspoon **chilli powder**

¼ teaspoon **turmeric**

1 **red pepper**, cored, deseeded and chopped

4 **garlic cloves**, crushed

2 tablespoons **coriander leaves**

good

fast

star

A perfect accompaniment to Mushroom Korma (see page 156) or Mung Dhal (see page 161).

1 Heat the oil in a large saucepan, add the onion and fry gently for 2–3 minutes until it begins to soften. Add the cumin and mustard seeds and fry, stirring, for another 2 minutes.

2 Add the tomatoes, chilli, mushrooms and peas. Stir and cook for 2 minutes.

3 Add the chilli powder and turmeric, mix well, then cook, uncovered, for 5–7 minutes.

4 Add the pepper, garlic and coriander and fry for 5 minutes until the mixture is quite dry. Best eaten hot.

onion bhajis

These spicy bhajis are delicious served hot with chutney.

PREP

10

COOK

10*

SERVES

4

snack

quick

hot

1 **onion**, halved and thinly sliced

5 tablespoons **gram flour**

1 tablespoon **vegetable oil**

2 teaspoons **salt**

1 teaspoon **sugar**

1 teaspoon **lemon juice**

1 teaspoon ground **cumin**

1 **green chilli**, deseeded and finely chopped

1 tablespoon chopped **coriander**

¾ teaspoon **baking powder**

2–3 tablespoons **water**

vegetable oil, for deep-frying

1 Mix all the ingredients together in a bowl (apart from the oil for deep-frying) then leave the mixture to rest for 10 minutes.

2 Heat enough oil in a saucepan to deep-fry the bhajis (it is hot enough when a cube of bread browns within 30 seconds). Drop spoonfuls of the mixture into the oil and deep-fry in batches for 1–2 minutes, until golden. Eat hot.

* + standing

meals for mates

375 g (12 oz) waxy **potatoes**, peeled

½ small **onion**, very thinly sliced

1 tablespoon chopped **dill**

½ teaspoon **salt**

15 g (½ oz) **self-raising flour**

1 **egg**, beaten

vegetable oil, for frying

Mushroom sauce:

25 g (1 oz) **butter**

2 **shallots**, chopped

1 **garlic clove**, crushed

375 g (12 oz) **button mushrooms**

2 tablespoons chopped **dill**

6 tablespoons **soured cream**

6 tablespoons **horseradish sauce**

salt and **pepper**

PREP

COOK

SERVES

super

crisp

feast

potato cakes with creamy mushrooms

These delicious potato cakes provide a lovely crisp base for the creamy mushrooms. A perfect combination.

1 Grate the potatoes very finely and squeeze out any excess liquid. Tip into a large bowl and stir in the onion, dill, salt and flour. Mix in the egg until it is all combined.

2 Make the mushroom sauce by melting the butter in a frying pan and fry the shallots and garlic for 5 minutes. Add the mushrooms and fry for 5–6 minutes until golden. Take off the heat and stir in the dill, soured cream, horseradish sauce and a dash of salt and pepper. Keep warm.

3 Heat the oil in a large frying pan. Divide the potato mixture into 8 balls then press flat into cakes. Fry in batches for 3–4 minutes on each side until golden then drain on kitchen paper.

4 Dish up the potato cakes, dollop on the mushroom sauce, sprinkle with pepper and tuck in.

red pepper and bean cakes

Stuff these crispy bean cakes into warm pitta bread, dollop on the lemon mayo and serve with salad – a fantastic snack.

1 Cook the French beans in a saucepan of boiling water for 1–2 minutes until soft but crunchy, then drain.

2 Meanwhile, heat the oil in a frying pan and fry the pepper, garlic and chilli powder for 2 minutes.

3 Pour the mixture into a blender or food processor and add the red kidney beans, breadcrumbs and egg yolk. Blend quickly until the ingredients are coarsely chopped. Add the French beans and a dash of salt and pepper and blend until the ingredients are just mixed.

4 Pour the mixture into a bowl and divide into 8. Using lightly floured hands, shape into little 'cakes'.

5 Make the lemon mayo by mixing the mayonnaise with the lemon rind and juice and a good dash of salt and pepper.

6 Heat the oil for frying in a large frying pan and fry the cakes for about 3 minutes on each side until crisp and golden. Dollop on the lemon mayonnaise and serve with a green salad.

pals

saucy

fresh

75 g (3 oz) **green beans**, trimmed and roughly chopped

2 tablespoons **vegetable oil**

1 **red pepper**, cored, deseeded and cut into cubes

4 **garlic cloves**, crushed

2 teaspoons mild **chilli powder**

425 g (14 oz) can **red kidney beans**, drained and rinsed

75 g (3 oz) **breadcrumbs**

1 **egg yolk**

plain flour, for dusting

vegetable oil, for frying

salt and **pepper**

Lemon mayonnaise:

4 tablespoons **mayonnaise**

finely grated rind of 1 **lemon**

1 teaspoon **lemon juice**

salt and **pepper**

300 g (10 oz) **tofu**, cut into cubes

15 large **button mushrooms**

2 tablespoons **sesame oil**

6 tablespoons **soy sauce**

4 tablespoons **red wine vinegar**

2 teaspoons grated **root ginger**

2 **garlic cloves**, crushed

2 tablespoons **clear honey**

4 tablespoons **water**

2 tablespoons **sweet chilli sauce**

Peanut sauce:

1 tablespoon **vegetable oil**

1 **garlic clove**, crushed

1 **red chilli**, deseeded and finely chopped

4 tablespoons **crunchy peanut butter**

1 tablespoon **lime juice**

15 g (½ oz) **creamed coconut**

PREP

COOK

SERVES

tangy

fancy

yum!

mushroom and tofu kebabs

What a great mix of flavours – this is one dish you will want to make again and again.

1 Thread the tofu and mushrooms alternately on to 8 skewers. To make the glaze, mix together the rest of the kebab ingredients in a saucepan and bring to the boil. Boil rapidly until the sauce is thick and glossy and reduced in volume by half. Leave to cool slightly.

2 Make the peanut sauce. Heat the oil in a saucepan and gently fry the garlic and chilli for 3 minutes. Gradually stir in the rest of the ingredients. Bring to the boil, stirring constantly, and add enough boiling water to make a smooth pouring sauce. Turn off the heat, cover and keep warm.

3 Brush the kebabs all over with the glaze and cook for 8–10 minutes under a hot grill, turning and basting often, until golden and tender. Serve hot with the peanut sauce to dip into.

couscous with grilled vegetables

This North African-inspired dish tastes delicious – and it's good for you, too!

cheap

mates

best

1 Grill the aubergine slices under a medium grill for 5 minutes on each side. Grill the garlic slices for 30 seconds on each side.

2 Grill the chillies and the pepper whole – the chillies for about 5 minutes and the pepper for 10 minutes. Turn frequently until they are charred all over.

3 Meanwhile, cut the red onions into wedges and grill for 5 minutes on each side. Grill the courgette slices for 4 minutes on each side.

4 Put the couscous in a large bowl, cover with boiling water and leave for 5 minutes.

5 When they are cool, peel and deseed the chillies and red pepper. Roughly chop all the vegetables and add them to the couscous. Add the spices, salt and pepper and mix well. Drizzle with olive oil and tuck in.

1 **aubergine**, sliced

2 **garlic cloves**, sliced

2 **green chillies**

1 **red pepper**

2 **red onions**

1 **courgette**, sliced

125 g (4 oz) **couscous**

½ teaspoon **cumin**

½ teaspoon **paprika**

pinch of dried **chilli flakes**

salt and **pepper**

3 tablespoons **olive oil**, to drizzle

2 small **butternut squash**

3 tablespoons **olive oil**

1 large **onion**, finely chopped

1 **garlic clove**, crushed

1 tablespoon chopped **thyme**

1 teaspoon ground **coriander**

50 g (2 oz) **breadcrumbs**

50 g (2 oz) **walnuts**, toasted and chopped

50 g (2 oz) **sun-dried tomatoes** in oil, drained and chopped

2 tablespoons **basil**, chopped

200 g (7 oz) **goats' cheese**, cut into 8 slices

salt and **pepper**

COOK

75

SERVES

4

fills

boozy

good

baked butternut squash

This stuffed squash makes a very filling dish. Just don't plan on doing anything too energetic after eating it …

1 Heat the oven to 190°C (375°F), Gas Mark 5.

2 Prick each butternut squash several times and bake in the oven for 35–45 minutes. Leave to cool.

3 Meanwhile, heat half the oil in a frying pan, add the onion, garlic, thyme and coriander and fry gently for 10 minutes. Heat the rest of the oil in another frying pan and fry the breadcrumbs for 4–5 minutes until crisp and golden.

4 Cut each squash in half lengthways and take out the seeds. Carefully scoop out the flesh, chop finely and tip into a bowl. Stir in the onion mixture, breadcrumbs, walnuts, tomatoes and basil and add a good dash of salt and pepper.

5 Divide the filling among the squash shells and top with the cheese. Bake in the oven for 30 minutes then serve hot with a green salad.

walnut-stuffed aubergines

The crunchy nuts give the baked aubergine a great texture. All you need is a nicely dressed green salad to go with this.

PREP

30

COOK

40

SERVES

4

share

tasty

smart

6 tablespoons **brown rice**

2 large **aubergines**

2 tablespoons **olive oil**

1 **onion**, chopped

2 **garlic cloves**, crushed

3 **celery sticks**, chopped

175 g (6 oz) **mushrooms**, chopped

50 g (2 oz) **walnuts**, ground

1 tablespoon **tomato purée**

2 tablespoons chopped **parsley**

75 g (3 oz) **Cheddar cheese**, grated

salt and **pepper**

1 Heat the oven to 190°C (375°F), Gas Mark 5.

2 Cook the rice according to the packet instructions.

3 Meanwhile, prick the aubergines all over, cut them in half lengthways and place them on a baking sheet with the cut side facing down. Bake in the oven for 30 minutes.

4 Heat the oil in a pan, add the onion and fry until soft. Add the garlic and celery and fry for 5 minutes. Add the mushrooms and fry, stirring, for 3 minutes. Stir in the rice, walnuts, tomato purée, parsley and salt and pepper, then turn off the heat.

5 Carefully scoop the flesh from the aubergines without breaking the skins. Chop the flesh finely and mix it with the fried mixture. Pile the mixture into the aubergine skins, sprinkle with the cheese and cook under a hot grill until bubbling.

750 g (1½ lb) **baby leeks**, trimmed and halved

2 tablespoons **hazelnut oil**

4 tablespoons **vegetable stock**

15 g (½ oz) **butter**

125 g (4 oz) **dolcelatte cheese**, crumbled

2 tablespoons **hazelnuts**, chopped

salt and **pepper**

COOK

35

SERVES

4

super

fab!

posh

leeks baked with blue cheese

The emphasis here is on simplicity – just let all the different flavours come out naturally.

1 Heat the oven to 200°C (400°F), Gas Mark 6.

2 In a bowl toss the leeks with the oil and place in a large roasting tin with the stock. Bake in the oven for 15 minutes.

3 Dot the leeks with the butter, cheese and nuts, then pop back in the oven and cook for another 15–20 minutes until the leeks are tender and the cheese has melted and is golden. Sprinkle with salt and pepper and eat straight away.

balsamic braised leeks and peppers

Cooking the peppers and leeks in balsamic vinegar gives them a delightfully soft, mellow quality and will really get your taste buds going.

1 Heat the oil in saucepan and cook the leeks and peppers very gently, covered, for 10 minutes.

2 Add the vinegar and cook for a further 10 minutes without a lid. The vegetables should be brown from the vinegar and all the liquid should have evaporated.

3 Add a good dash of salt and pepper then stir in the parsley and dish up.

PREP

5

COOK

20

SERVES

4

party

great

light

1½ tablespoons **olive oil**

2 **leeks**, cut into 1 cm (½ inch) pieces

1 **orange pepper**, cored, deseeded and cut into 1 cm (½ inch) chunks

1 **red pepper**, cored, deseeded and cut into 1 cm (½ inch) chunks

3 tablespoons **balsamic vinegar**

1 handful of chopped **parsley**

salt and **pepper**

125 g (4 oz) **red lentils**

400 g (13 oz) canned **tomatoes**

1 **garlic clove**, crushed

½ teaspoon dried **oregano**

pinch of ground **nutmeg**

150 ml (¼ pint) **vegetable stock**

1 tablespoon **vegetable oil**

250 g (8 oz) **aubergine**, sliced

1 **onion**

Cheese topping:

1 **egg**

150 g (5 oz) **soft cheese**

nutmeg

salt and **pepper**

PREP

10

COOK

45

SERVES

4

beer

fills

basic

lentil moussaka

This vegetarian adaptation of a classic Greek dish makes a really good winter's lunch.

1 Put the lentils in a saucepan with the tomatoes, garlic, oregano, nutmeg and stock, then simmer for 20 minutes.

2 Meanwhile, heat the oil and lightly fry the aubergine with the onion until brown.

3 Heat the oven to 200°C (400°F), Gas Mark 6.

4 Layer the aubergines and lentil mixture alternately in an ovenproof dish.

5 Make the topping. In a bowl, beat together the egg, cheese and nutmeg with a good dash of salt and pepper. Pour over the moussaka and cook in the oven for about 20–25 minutes. A Greek delight!

mushroom stroganoff

The perfect hassle-free meal for a retro 70s night in.

1 Heat the oil in a nonstick frying pan, add the onion, celery and garlic and cook for 5 minutes. Add the mushrooms and paprika and cook for another 5 minutes. Pour in the stock and cook for a further 10 minutes or until the liquid is reduced by half.

2 Stir in the soured cream with a dash of salt and pepper and cook over a medium heat for 5 minutes. Dish up on a bed of boiled rice.

PREP

10

COOK

25

SERVES

4

feast

hot

great

1 tablespoon **vegetable oil**

1 large **onion**, thinly sliced

4 **celery sticks**, thinly sliced

2 **garlic cloves**, crushed

600 g (1 lb 3 oz) **mixed mushrooms**, roughly chopped

2 teaspoons **paprika**

250 ml (8 fl oz) **vegetable stock**

150 ml (¼ pint) **soured cream**

salt and **pepper**

2 tablespoons **olive oil**

375 g (12 oz) **cherry tomatoes**

1 **onion**, finely chopped

2 **garlic cloves**, crushed

3 tablespoons **sun-dried tomato purée**

325 g (11 oz) **puff pastry**, thawed if frozen

beaten **egg**, to glaze

Crème fraîche pesto:

150 g (5 oz) **crème fraîche**

2 tablespoons **pesto**

salt and **pepper**

PREP

10

COOK

18

SERVES

4

fab!

crisp

snack

cherry tomato tartlets

If these aren't gobbled up straight away – which is unlikely as they taste so good – then they are just as tasty cold.

1 Heat the oven to 220°C (425°F), Gas Mark 7.

2 Grease a baking sheet and sprinkle with water. Halve 150 g (5 oz) of the tomatoes.

3 Heat the oil in a frying pan, add the onion and fry for about 3 minutes until soft. Take the pan off the heat, add the garlic and tomato purée, then stir in all the tomatoes.

4 Roll out the pastry on a lightly floured surface and cut out four 12 cm (5 inch) circles using a small bowl as a guide. Place on the baking sheet and make a shallow cut 1 cm (½ inch) from the edge of each circle to make a rim. Brush the rims with beaten egg. Pile the tomato mixture on to the centres of the pastries, making sure the mixture stays within the rims.

5 Bake in the oven for about 15 minutes until the pastry has risen and is golden.

6 Meanwhile, mix together the crème fraîche, pesto and salt and pepper in a bowl so that the crème fraîche is streaked with the pesto. Pop the tartlets on to a plate and add a generous dollop of the crème fraîche pesto. Superb!

roasted vegetable and feta tart

Invite your friends round and catch up on the gossip while you snack on this.

telly

share

tasty

450 g (14½ oz) ready-rolled **shortcrust pastry**, thawed if frozen

vegetable oil, for greasing

Filling:

1 **red pepper**, cored, deseeded and cut into thick strips

1 **onion**, cut into wedges

2 **courgettes**, cut into thick slices

3 **tomatoes**, halved

2 **garlic cloves**, chopped

3 tablespoons **olive oil**

4 small **rosemary** sprigs

125 g (4 oz) **feta cheese**, crumbled

2 tablespoons **Parmesan cheese**, grated

salt and **pepper**

1 Heat the oven to 200°C (400°F), Gas Mark 6.

2 Unfold the pastry and lay it over the inside of a greased 23 cm (9 inch) flan tin. Push gently into place and prick the base with a fork. Cover with a piece of greaseproof paper and fill the bottom with a layer of cheap dried beans, such as butter beans.

3 Bake in the oven for 10 minutes. Remove the paper and beans and bake for another 10–12 minutes until crisp and golden.

4 Meanwhile, to make the filling mix all the vegetables in a roasting tin. Add the garlic, oil and rosemary with a good dash of salt and pepper. Stir the mixture to coat the vegetables evenly and roast in the oven for 35 minutes.

5 Fill the pastry case with the vegetables, arrange the feta on top and sprinkle with Parmesan. Return to the oven for 10 minutes, then serve.

4 tablespoons **vegetable oil**

1 **onion**, sliced

1 **celery stick**, thinly sliced

1 **parsnip**, sliced

425 g (14 oz) can **mixed beans**, rinsed and drained

425 g (14 oz) can **baked beans**

250 ml (8 fl oz) **beer**

250 ml (8 fl oz) **vegetable stock**

4 tablespoons chopped **herbs** (such as rosemary, marjoram or thyme)

150 g (5 oz) **self-raising flour**

75 g (3 oz) **vegetable suet**

2 tablespoons **mustard**

salt and **pepper**

PREP

COOK

SERVES

boozy

fills

bean and beer casserole

Healthy, hearty and hot, here's a great supper to make for your friends when you are all feeling in need of good food.

1 Heat the oil in a large saucepan and fry the onion, celery and parsnip for 3 minutes. Add the mixed beans, baked beans, beer, stock and 3 tablespoons of the herbs. Bring to the boil and let the mixture bubble, uncovered, for 8–10 minutes until slightly thickened then pour into a casserole dish.

2 Meanwhile, mix the flour, suet, mustard, remaining herbs and a little salt and pepper in a bowl with 8–9 tablespoons of cold water to make a soft dough.

3 Put about 8 rounded spoonfuls of the dough into the casserole, spread out evenly, and cover with a lid. Cook for 10 minutes until the dumplings are light and fluffy. Serve straight away.

pumpkin goulash

Packed with Hungarian flavour, this cheap and tasty pumpkin and lentil casserole can be made in advance and reheated when needed. Serve with chunky slices of bread.

1 Heat the oven to 180°C (350°F), Gas Mark 4.

2 Heat the oil in a casserole dish, add the onion and fry for 5 minutes, until lightly browned. Add the red pepper, garlic, paprika and caraway seeds and cook, stirring, for 1 minute.

3 Add the pumpkin, carrot, lentils, stock, tomato purée, sugar and salt and pepper. Bring to the boil, cover and cook in the oven for 1 hour.

4 Spoon the goulash into bowls then top with a spoonful of crème fraîche and a sprinkling of paprika.

PREP

10

COOK

70

SERVES
2

tasty

great

beer

1 tablespoon **vegetable oil**

1 **onion**, chopped

1 **red pepper**, cored, deseeded and cut into chunks

1 **garlic clove**, crushed

2 teaspoons **paprika**

1 teaspoon **caraway seeds**

375 g (12 oz) **pumpkin** or **butternut squash**, thickly sliced and deseeded

1 large **carrot**, thickly sliced

75 g (3 oz) **red lentils**, rinsed

450 ml (¾ pint) **vegetable stock**

4 teaspoons **tomato purée**

1 teaspoon **sugar**

salt and **pepper**

To top:

4 tablespoons **crème fraîche** or **natural yogurt**

paprika

500 g (1 lb) dried **red** or **white kidney beans**, soaked overnight, drained and rinsed

2 **celery sticks**, halved

2 **bay leaves**

4 **parsley** sprigs

4 tablespoons **olive oil**

500 g (1 lb) **onions**, chopped

5 **garlic cloves**, crushed

2 **red chillies**, deseeded and chopped

4 **red peppers**, cored, deseeded and chopped

1 tablespoon **paprika**

large handful of mixed **herbs** (such as mint, parsley or coriander), roughly chopped

salt and **pepper**

Tomato sauce:

1 kg (2 lb) can chopped **tomatoes**

2 tablespoons **olive oil**

4 sprigs **parsley**

1 tablespoon **sugar**

PREP

COOK

SERVES

8

spicy

fresh

good

bean tagine

Tagine is the traditional name for both a North African cooking pot and the thick stew cooked slowly within it. Definitely one to try!

1 Boil the beans in a large saucepan of water for 10 minutes then drain. Tie the celery, bay leaves and parsley together with string. Cover the beans with cold water, add the celery and herbs and simmer for about 1 hour until the beans are tender. Drain, keeping the cooking liquid, and chuck out the celery and herbs.

2 Meanwhile, make the tomato sauce. Empty the tomatoes into a saucepan, add the oil, parsley and sugar and bring to the boil then simmer, uncovered, for 20 minutes until thick.

3 Heat the oven to 150°C (300°F), Gas Mark 2.

4 Heat the oil in a large casserole dish. Add the onions, garlic, chillies, red peppers and paprika and cook gently for 5 minutes. Stir in the beans, the tomato sauce and enough of the cooking liquid to just cover the beans. Sprinkle with salt and pepper, cover and cook in the oven for 1½ hours, stirring occasionally.

5 Stir in the mint, parsley and coriander and dish up straight away.

* + soaking

spanish vegetable stew

PREP

15

This delicious stew is packed with a wonderful assortment of vegetables. If you prefer, you can use parsnips, celeriac, shredded greens or courgettes instead.

COOK

45

SERVES

4

1 Heat the oil in a large saucepan. Add the onions, garlic, paprika and peppers and fry gently for 6–8 minutes until soft and brown.

2 Meanwhile, melt the butter in a frying pan and fry the breadcrumbs for 2 minutes or until golden.

3 Add the potatoes, tomato purée and stock to the pepper mixture and bring to the boil. Turn down the heat, cover the pan and simmer gently for about 30 minutes until the vegetables are tender.

4 Stir in the butter beans and spinach or spring greens and cook for 3–4 minutes until the beans have heated through and the spinach has wilted. Sprinkle with the breadcrumbs and serve.

saucy

pals

green

3 tablespoons **vegetable oil**

2 **onions**, thinly sliced

3 **garlic cloves**, sliced

1 tablespoon **paprika**

1 **green pepper**, cored, deseeded and sliced

1 **red pepper**, cored, deseeded and sliced

25 g (1 oz) **butter**

50 g (2 oz) **breadcrumbs**

500 g (1 lb) **potatoes**, cut into chunks

2 tablespoons **tomato purée**

600 ml (1 pint) **vegetable stock**

2 × 400 g (13 oz) cans **butter beans**, rinsed and drained

200 g (7 oz) **baby spinach** or **shredded spring greens**

175 g (6 oz) split **red lentils**

600 ml (1 pint) boiling **water**

3 tablespoons **vegetable oil**

1 large **onion**, finely chopped

1 large **green pepper**, cored, deseeded and cut into cubes

175 g (6 oz) **mushrooms**, sliced

1 teaspoon **chilli powder**

½ teaspoon **Tabasco sauce**

1 teaspoon **paprika**

1 tablespoon **tomato purée**

2 tablespoon **soy sauce**

salt and **pepper**

Topping:

25 g (1 oz) **breadcrumbs**

25 g (1 oz) **pine nuts**, chopped

25 g (1 oz) **pumpkin seeds**

50 g (2 oz) **Cheddar cheese**, grated

184 meals for mates

PREP

10

COOK

60

SERVES

4

star

fun

fancy

red lentil and pepper bake

This firm favourite has a wonderfully deep and rich flavour. Instead of using peppers and mushrooms, try adding any combination of courgettes, aubergines, tomatoes and celery.

1 Put the lentils into a saucepan and cover with the boiling water. Bring to the boil, then turn down the heat and simmer gently for about 20 minutes, stirring occasionally, until the lentils are tender and all the water has been absorbed.

2 Heat the oven to 190°C (375°F), Gas Mark 5. Lightly oil a large ovenproof dish.

3 Heat the rest of the oil in a large saucepan and fry the onion until soft but not coloured. Add the green pepper and mushrooms, turn up the heat and fry for about 10 minutes to colour the vegetables slightly.

4 Add the lentils, chilli powder, Tabasco, paprika, tomato purée, soy and salt and pepper. Stir well, then pour into the ovenproof dish.

5 Mix the topping ingredients together and sprinkle over the lentil mixture. Bake in the oven for about 30 minutes, until bubbling hot. Delicious.

hot spicy stew with potatoes and cauliflower

Stews can be light and subtle or richly spiced and substantial. The possibilities are endless.

1 Soak the lentils in a bowl of water for 15 minutes, then run under cold running water, drain and tip into a large saucepan with half the stock. Bring to the boil, then turn down the heat and simmer for 30 minutes until the lentils are soft and all the liquid has been absorbed.

2 Meanwhile, heat the oil in a large saucepan, add the onion and fry over a low heat for about 8 minutes, stirring often. Add the potatoes, cauliflower and garlic and cook for 1 minute. Stir in the turmeric, mustard and fennel seeds and the chillies.

3 Add the rest of the stock and the soaked saffron and bring to the boil. Turn down the heat and cook gently for 10–15 minutes until the vegetables are almost cooked.

4 Mash the lentils to make a thick purée, leaving a few whole. Add the coconut cream and coriander and mix well. Pour on to the vegetables and mix well again. Add a good dash of salt and pepper and cook gently until the vegetables are tender and the flavours delightfully combined.

tangy

super

hot

375 g (12 oz) **lentils** or **split peas**

1.8 litres (3 pints) **vegetable stock**

3 tablespoons **vegetable oil**

2 large **onions**, cut into wedges

1–1.25 kg (2–2½ lb) **potatoes**, cut into chunks

1 **cauliflower**, cut into florets and stalks removed

3–4 **garlic cloves**, crushed

2 teaspoons **turmeric**

2 tablespoons **mustard seeds**

1–2 tablespoons **fennel seeds**

1–2 **green chillies**, deseeded and chopped

1 teaspoon **saffron threads**, soaked in 2 tablespoons warm water

125 g (4 oz) **coconut cream**

1 tablespoon chopped **coriander**

salt and **pepper**

25 g (1 oz) dried **chickpeas**

25 g (1 oz) dried **haricot beans**

25 g (1 oz) dried **black-eyed beans**

25 g (1 oz) dried **red kidney beans**

15 g (½ oz) **butter**

1 small **onion**, chopped

1 **carrot**, sliced

1 **celery stick**, chopped

1 **garlic clove**, crushed

250 g (8 oz) can **tomatoes**

½ teaspoon dried **mixed herbs**

75 g (3 oz) **Cheddar cheese**, grated

salt and **pepper**

PREP

COOK

SERVES

mates

moist

beer

vegetarian hotpot

Packed with goodness, this tasty hotpot is great for sharing with friends. Even the confirmed carnivores will love it.

1 Put the chickpeas, haricot beans and black-eyed beans in a large bowl and cover with cold water. Put the kidney beans in a separate bowl and cover with water. Soak overnight.

2 Drain and tip the chickpeas, haricot beans and black-eyed beans into a saucepan; put the kidney beans in a separate saucepan (to stop the others from turning pink). Cover the pulses with fresh cold water. Bring to the boil, boil for 10 minutes, then cover and simmer for 40 minutes or until tender. Drain, rinse under cold water, then drain again.

3 Melt the butter in a saucepan, add the onion, carrot and celery and fry until soft. Stir in the garlic, pulses, tomatoes, herbs and a dash of salt and pepper.

4 Bring to the boil, cover and simmer for 1–1¼ hours, adding a little water if the mixture becomes too dry. Sprinkle the cheese over the top, and serve with rice.

* + soaking

rich vegetable pie

This rich-tasting pie will really impress your friends. Just keep the red wine flowing and enjoy the evening.

PREP

30

COOK

80

SERVES

6

sexy

fab!

share

1 Heat half the oil in a frying pan, add the mushrooms and garlic and fry for 3–4 minutes. Remove from the pan and put on one side. Add the rest of the oil to the pan and fry the onions, parsnips, carrots and herbs for 10 minutes.

2 Add the wine and boil rapidly for 3 minutes. Stir in the tomatoes, stock, tomato purée and soy sauce. Bring to the boil, cover and simmer for 30 minutes.

3 Add the garlicky mushrooms and some salt and pepper, then tip into a 1.75 litre (3 pint) or similar pie dish.

4 Heat the oven to 220°C (425°F), Gas Mark 7.

5 Roll out the pastry to a shape just larger than the pie dish and then carefully lay it over the top of the pie. Trim the edges with a knife and press down well to seal the pastry. Prick some holes in the lid with a fork and brush on the egg white to make a glaze.

6 Bake in the oven for 20 minutes, then turn down the temperature to 200°C (400°F), Gas Mark 6, and bake for another 15 minutes.

4 tablespoons **vegetable oil**

500 g (1 lb) **button mushrooms**, halved

2 **garlic cloves**, crushed

250 g (8 oz) **baby onions**, halved

250 g (8 oz) **parsnips**, chopped

250 g (8 oz) **carrots**, chopped

2 tablespoons chopped **thyme**

1 tablespoon chopped **sage**

300 ml (½ pint) **red wine**

400 g (13 oz) can chopped **tomatoes**

150 ml (¼ pint) **vegetable stock**

2 tablespoons **tomato purée**

2 tablespoons **soy sauce**

425 g (14 oz) **puff pastry**, thawed if frozen

salt and **pepper**

1 **egg white**, to glaze

3 tablespoons **vegetable oil**

1 **garlic clove**, peeled

275 g (9 oz) **tomatoes**, cut into wedges

1 **green pepper**, cored, deseeded and chopped

325 g (11 oz) can **sweetcorn**

pinch of grated **nutmeg**

2 tablespoons unsalted **peanuts**, chopped

4–5 tablespoons **double cream**

1 medium **egg yolk**

2 medium **egg whites**

salt and **pepper**

PREP

COOK

SERVES

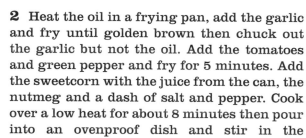

sweetcorn and tomato bake

Creamy, nutty and tasty, this is delicious with warm, crusty French bread.

1 Heat the oven to 220°C (425°F), Gas Mark 7.

2 Heat the oil in a frying pan, add the garlic and fry until golden brown then chuck out the garlic but not the oil. Add the tomatoes and green pepper and fry for 5 minutes. Add the sweetcorn with the juice from the can, the nutmeg and a dash of salt and pepper. Cook over a low heat for about 8 minutes then pour into an ovenproof dish and stir in the peanuts.

3 Mix the cream with the egg yolk and stir into the vegetable mixture. Whisk the egg whites until they make stiff peaks, then fold into the vegetable mixture with a metal spoon. Cook in the oven for 25–30 minutes.

spinach and cheese filo pie

PREP

15

COOK

65

SERVES

6

Although feta is the traditional cheese to use in this Greek delicacy, this recipe combines two other cheeses for a fuller flavour. Serve hot or cold.

1   Heat the oven to 190°C (375°F), Gas Mark 5.

2   Boil the spinach in a pan of water for a few minutes. Drain and squeeze well. Chop roughly and put into a large bowl.

3   Heat the oil in a frying pan and fry the onion and garlic until soft. Add to the spinach. Leave to cool, then add the feta, ricotta, Parmesan and parsley. Mash together, then stir in the egg and a dash of nutmeg and pepper and mix well.

4   Melt the butter and grease a deep ovenproof dish. Use the remainder to brush each sheet of pastry as you need it. Line the dish with 2–3 sheets of pastry, pushing it into the sides and letting the extra hang over the edges. Fold 6 sheets in half lengthways and place over the dish, angling them all slightly so that the edges look like the points of a star.

5   Spoon in the spinach mixture. Lay two sheets of filo pastry on top, tucking them in. Bring the overhanging sheets over the top layer of pastry, then place the last 3 sheets on top, scrunching them up to fit into the dish. Brush with butter, then bake for 45–60 minutes until crisp. Cool slightly, then remove from the tin.

super

smart

party

500 g (1 lb) frozen **spinach**, thawed

2 tablespoons **olive oil**

1 large **onion**, finely chopped

3 **garlic cloves**, crushed

75 g (3 oz) **feta cheese**, crumbled

75 g (3 oz) **ricotta** or **cottage cheese**

50 g (2 oz) **Parmesan cheese**, grated

2 tablespoons finely chopped **parsley**

3 **eggs**, beaten

grated **nutmeg**

75 g (3 oz) **butter**

12–14 sheets thawed **filo pastry**, each sheet 32 × 17.5 cm (12⅛ × 7½ inches)

black pepper

40 g (1½ oz) **butter**

1 **onion**, chopped

1 **celery stick**, chopped

250 g (8 oz) mixed **nuts**, coarsely chopped

3 large **tomatoes**, skinned and chopped

175 g (6 oz) **breadcrumbs**

1 teaspoon dried **mixed herbs**

¼ teaspoon **chilli powder**

2 **eggs**, lightly beaten

salt and **pepper**

PREP

30

COOK

70

SERVES

4

fills

mates

star

crumbly nut roast

Why not make a traditional Sunday lunch for your friends? With roasted potatoes, freshly cooked vegetables and gravy this is a real treat.

1 Heat the oven to 220°C (425°F), Gas Mark 7. Grease a 500 g (1 lb) tin and line the base with greaseproof paper.

2 Melt the butter in a large saucepan and fry the onion and celery for 5 minutes without letting it brown. Add the nuts, tomatoes, breadcrumbs, mixed herbs, chilli powder and a dash of salt and pepper. Add the eggs and mix together well, then taste and add more salt and pepper or herbs if it needs it.

3 Spoon the mixture into the prepared tin, cover with foil and bake in the oven for 50–60 minutes.

4 Take off the foil, turn the loaf out on to a dish and serve with potatoes.

roasted vegetables with garlic dip

Roasting vegetables draws out their natural sweetness and intense flavour, just make sure you cut the vegetables into similar size pieces so they cook evenly.

PREP

25

COOK

85

SERVES

4

share

tasty

snack

1 Heat the oven to 200°C (425°F), Gas Mark 7.

2 Boil the whole head of garlic in a saucepan of boiling water for 5 minutes. Drain and pat dry on kitchen paper.

3 Put all the vegetables and herbs in a large roasting tin, placing the garlic in the middle. Sprinkle generously with salt and pepper and stir in the oil to coat the vegetables. Cover the tin with foil and bake in the oven for 50 minutes. Remove the foil and bake for another 30 minutes.

4 Take the garlic out of the pan. Carefully peel and throw away the skin then mash the garlic flesh with a fork. Put the bread in a bowl, add the milk and soak for 5 minutes.

5 Place the bread and garlic in a blender or food processor and blend to make a smooth paste. Gradually add the oil a little at a time until well mixed, then add a good dash of salt and pepper.

6 Dip the roasted vegetables into the garlic sauce and tuck in.

1 large head **garlic**

2 large **onions**, cut into wedges

8 small **carrots**, quartered

8 small **parsnips**, cut into chunks

12 small **potatoes**

2 heads **fennel**, sliced thickly

4 **rosemary** sprigs

4 **thyme** sprigs

6 tablespoons **olive oil**

salt and **pepper**

Garlic dip:

1 large slice **bread**

4 tablespoons **milk**

75 ml (3 fl oz) **olive oil**

salt and **pepper**

cheese fondue

1 **garlic clove**, cut in half

200 ml (7 fl oz) **white wine**

1 teaspoon **lemon juice**

300 g (10 oz) **Emmental cheese**, grated

300 g (10 oz) **Gruyère cheese**, grated

1 tablespoon **cornflour**

3 tablespoons **Kirsch**

pinch of **white pepper**

pinch of ground **nutmeg**

pinch of **paprika**

cubes of **French bread**, to dip

PREP

10

COOK

20

SERVES

4

beer

fast

best

Fondues – a favourite in the 1970s – are a very sociable way to eat. They are enjoying a revival now, so why not try this classic dish?

1 Rub the inside of a fondue pot with the garlic, then throw away the garlic. Pour the wine into the pot with the lemon juice and cook gently, stirring over a low heat on the stove. Gradually add the cheese, stirring in a figure-of-eight motion, until all the cheese is mixed in.

2 Blend the cornflour and Kirsch together and as soon as the cheese mixture begins to bubble, add to the fondue. Continue to cook gently for 2–3 minutes and add the pepper, nutmeg and paprika.

3 Move the fondue pot to the table and keep warm on a burner. Dip in cubes of French bread and enjoy.

beer and onion fondue

PREP
10

COOK

20

SERVES

2

fun

gooey

boozy

Beer and cheese work together really well, whether served separately as a pint and a ploughman's or mixed together in a fondue.

3 tablespoons **butter**

1 **onion**, finely chopped

300 ml (½ pint) **beer**

250 g (8 oz) **Cheddar cheese**, grated

1 **garlic clove**, crushed

3 tablespoons **cornflour**

½ teaspoon **mustard powder**

black pepper

To dip:

cubes of **French bread**

pickled onions

1 Heat 1 tablespoon of the butter in a frying pan. Add the onion and gently fry until soft but not brown.

2 Put the beer, cheese, crushed garlic and onion in a fondue pot. Cook gently, stirring, over a low heat on the stove, until the cheese has melted. Stir in the rest of the butter.

3 Blend the cornflour and mustard in a little water and add to the fondue pot. Cook until thick, stirring all the time. Sprinkle with pepper.

4 Move the fondue pot to the table and keep warm on a burner. Serve with cubes of French bread and pickled onions to dip into the fondue.

sweet treats

75 ml (3 fl oz) unsweetened **pineapple juice**

50 g (2 oz) **clear honey**

125 g (4 oz) canned **lychees**

1 small **pineapple**, skinned, cored and cut into cubes

125 g (4 oz) fresh or drained canned **cherries**, pitted

8 **kiwifruit**, peeled and thinly sliced

125 g (4 oz) **grapes**, seeded

50 g (2 oz) blanched **almonds**, halved

250 g (8 oz) **dessert apples**

250 g (8 oz) **bananas**

25 ml (1 fl oz) **lemon juice**

PREP

25*

COOK

0

SERVES

5

easy

moist

quick

fresh fruit salad

On a hot day there is nothing more refreshing than a deliciously cool fruit salad. It's best to leave the flavours to infuse overnight, but if you don't have time don't worry about it.

1 Stir together the pineapple juice and honey in a large bowl. When the honey has dissolved, tip in the lychees with their syrup. Add the pineapple, cherries, kiwifruit, grapes and almonds then cover and leave in the fridge overnight.

2 Just before serving, thinly slice the apples and peel and slice the bananas and stir them into the lemon juice so they are coated in the liquid. Add to the fruit salad, stir well and dish up straight away.

* + standing

summer fruit skewers

Stunning looking yet quick to prepare, these fruity kebabs taste delicious when dunked into the banana sauce. Don't eat the lemon grass though, as it's very chewy!

1 Cut the lemon grass stems in half lengthways, peel off the outer leaves and rinse well. Using the stems as skewers, thread the strawberries, nectarines and kiwifruit on to the lemon grass until all the stems have been filled. Put them on a plate and drizzle with lime juice.

2 Mash the banana then stir it into the fromage frais with the lime rind. Spoon the sauce into a small bowl and serve straight away with the fruit skewers.

PREP

10

COOK

0

SERVES

4

fancy

party

sexy

4 **lemon grass stalks**

400 g (13 oz) **strawberries**, halved

3 **nectarines** or **peaches**, halved, pitted and thickly sliced

4 **kiwifruit**, peeled and thickly sliced

grated rind and juice of 1 **lime**

1 **banana**

200 g (7 oz) **fromage frais**

bananas with toffee sauce

4 **bananas**

125 g (4 oz) **butter**

125 g (4 oz) **soft brown sugar**

125 ml (4 fl oz) **double cream**

dash of **lime juice**

vanilla **ice cream**, to serve

PREP

2

COOK

4

SERVES

4

gooey

yum!

share

A rather decadent pudding. If you don't like cooked bananas then you could just have the toffee sauce with ice cream ... or a chocolate brownie if you are feeling really devilish!

1 Peel the bananas and cut them in half lengthways. Melt the butter in a frying pan and fry the banana halves for about 30 seconds on each side, until lightly golden. Take the bananas out of the pan and keep them warm.

2 Stir the sugar and cream into the pan and heat gently to dissolve the sugar. Simmer gently for 2–3 minutes, until thickened, then add the lime juice.

3 Pop the bananas on to the plates, drizzle with the toffee sauce and add a generous scoop of ice cream. Sublime!

treacle sponge

A classic pudding! If you want to make a jam sponge, then simply use strawberry, raspberry, apricot or plum jam instead of the golden syrup.

1 Grease a 900 ml (1½ pint) pudding basin or similar ovenproof bowl. Beat the butter and sugar together in a bowl until really creamy, light and fluffy. Beat in the eggs, one at a time, adding a little of the flour with the second egg. Fold in the rest of the flour.

2 Spoon 4 tablespoons of golden syrup into the basin, then pour the sponge mixture on top. Cover the basin with foil, making a pleat across the centre so the pudding can rise. Put the basin in a large saucepan, with enough boiling water to come about halfway up the side of the basin. Boil for 1½–2 hours, adding more boiling water when necessary.

3 To make the sauce, heat the syrup and water in a small saucepan. Tip out the pudding on to a plate and pour the hot sauce over the top, then dish up with cream or ice cream. Fantastic!

PREP

25

COOK

120

SERVES
4

mates

hot

juicy

125 g (4 oz) **butter**, softened and cut into cubes, plus extra for greasing

125 g (4 oz) **caster sugar**

2 large **eggs**

125 g (4 oz) **self-raising flour**

4 tablespoons **golden syrup**

Treacle sauce:

4 tablespoons **golden syrup**

1 tablespoon **water**

1 kg (2 lb) **rhubarb**

125 g (4 oz) **caster sugar**

2 pieces **stem ginger**, chopped

2 tablespoons **stem ginger syrup**

Crumble:

250 g (8 oz) **plain flour**

125 g (4 oz) **butter**, softened and cut into cubes

25 g (1 oz) **caster sugar**

25 g (1 oz) **soft brown sugar**

PREP

20

COOK

40

SERVES

6

fruity

best

fills

rhubarb and ginger crumble

Crumbles are one of the simplest and most filling puddings you can make. If you want to leave out the ginger then add an extra tablespoon of sugar to take the bitter edge off the rhubarb.

1 Heat the oven to 190°C (375°F), Gas Mark 5.

2 Cut the ends off the rhubarb and remove the stringy skin. Cut the rhubarb into large chunks, put them in a large ovenproof dish and sprinkle with sugar. Add the stem ginger and stem ginger syrup and smooth out.

3 To make the crumble, pour the flour into a bowl and rub in the butter until the mixture looks like breadcrumbs. Mix in the caster sugar.

4 Cover the rhubarb with the crumble and press it down lightly. Sprinkle the surface with the brown sugar.

5 Bake the crumble in the oven for 40 minutes until golden brown, then serve hot with yogurt, whipped cream or vanilla ice cream.

plum crumble

Homely and comforting, this old-fashioned pudding is the perfect finale to a Sunday lunch. If you can't get plums then why not use gooseberries, apples, pears or peaches?

1 Heat the oven to 180°C (350°F), Gas Mark 4.

2 Put the plums, sugar and water into a saucepan and bring to the boil. Cover and simmer for 5 minutes, until just soft, then pour into a large ovenproof dish.

3 To make the topping, put the flour, oats and sugar into a bowl. Rub in the butter using your fingertips until the mixture looks like breadcrumbs. Mix in the seeds, then tip over the fruit.

4 Bake in the oven for 30 minutes until golden on top. It's delicious with a dollop of fromage frais.

PREP

15

COOK

35

SERVES

4

sweet

tasty

great

500 g (1 lb) **red plums**, halved and pitted

50 g (2 oz) **soft brown sugar**

3 tablespoons **water**

Crumble:

75 g (3 oz) **plain flour**

25 g (1 oz) **porridge oats**

50 g (2 oz) **soft brown sugar**

50 g (2 oz) **butter**, softened and cut into cubes

25 g (1 oz) **sunflower seeds**

25 g (1 oz) **sesame seeds**

100 g (3½ oz) **pudding rice**

450 ml (¾ pint) **milk**

450 ml (¾ pint) **cream**

75 g (2½ oz) **caster sugar**

½ teaspoon **nutmeg**

brown sugar, to sprinkle

baked rice pudding

A perfectly cooked rice pudding is a true delicacy, so it's worth knowing how to make it well. Pure bliss!

1 Preheat the oven to 180°C (350°F), Gas Mark 4.

2 Wash the rice under cold water and allow it to drain.

3 Bring the milk and cream to the boil, then add the rice, caster sugar and nutmeg.

fab!

4 Give the whole mixture a good stir, then pour into a lightly buttered oven dish, sprinkle with brown sugar, and sling it in the oven for about 15 minutes.

5 Then lower the temperature to 150°C (300°F), Gas Mark 2 and bake it for a further 1¼ hours.

easy

good

bread and butter pudding

10*

This is one of those puddings that is certain to bring back some childhood memories. Smothered in cream, ice cream or custard, it's always popular.

COOK

60

SERVES

4

40 g (1½ oz) **butter**

4 slices **white bread**, crusts removed

4 tablespoons **apricot jam**

25 g (1 oz) **mixed peel**

25 g (1 oz) **sultanas**

450 ml (¾ pint) **milk**

2 tablespoons **sugar**

2 **eggs**, beaten

1 Use 15 g (½ oz) of the butter to grease a 1.2 litre (2 pint) or similar ovenproof dish.

2 Butter the bread and spread with the apricot jam. Cut the bread into small triangles and layer them in the dish, sprinkling the mixed peel and sultanas between the layers.

3 Put the milk and sugar into a saucepan and heat until nearly boiling. Take off the heat and whisk in the eggs. Pour over the bread and leave to soak for 30 minutes.

4 Meanwhile, heat the oven to 180°C (350°F), Gas Mark 4.

5 Put the dish into a roasting tin and fill with water to halfway up the sides. Bake in the oven for 45 minutes, then turn up the heat to 190°C (375°F), Gas Mark 5 and cook for a further 10–15 minutes until crisp and golden on top. Cover in custard and enjoy!

cheap

super

basic

* + soaking

english trifle

8 **trifle sponge cakes**

2–3 tablespoons **seedless raspberry jam**

4–5 tablespoons **sherry**

4–5 tablespoons **brandy**

600 ml (1 pint) **milk**

4 **eggs**

25 g (1 oz) **caster sugar**

450 ml (¾ pint) **double cream**, whipped to soft peaks

PREP

10

COOK

10

SERVES

4

share

pals

fun

Trifle is always popular – maybe because of all the booze hidden within its creaminess. This is best made the day before so the flavours can infuse together overnight.

1 Cut the sponge cakes in half, spread them with jam and sandwich together. Cut each into 8 pieces and place them in the bottom of a glass bowl. Pour the sherry and brandy on top.

2 Heat the milk in a saucepan until it steams. Beat the eggs and sugar together until creamy then pour on the hot milk. Mix well, then tip back into the saucepan and heat gently, stirring, until the custard thickens. Leave the mixture to cool slightly, then pour it over the sponge cakes and leave until cold.

3 Spread the whipped cream over the top of the trifle and pop in the fridge until you fancy it.

no-bake lime and berry cheesecake

This tangy cheesecake couldn't be easier to make, yet the crumbly biscuit base, light, creamy filling and pretty berry topping are sure to tempt the taste buds.

1 To make the base, melt the butter and syrup in a saucepan then stir in the crushed biscuits. Mix well and press into the base of a greased 18 cm (7 inch) loose-bottomed tin or similar.

2 Beat the mascarpone in a bowl to soften, then stir in the fromage frais, sugar and lime rind. Gradually beat in the lime juice.

3 In another bowl, whisk the cream until it forms soft peaks, then fold it into the mascarpone mixture. Spoon the creamy filling on to the biscuit base and swirl the top with the back of a spoon. Pop into the fridge for at least 3 hours to chill.

4 Remove the cheesecake from the tin and decorate with the berries. A real delight!

* + chilling

PREP

20*

COOK

0

SERVES

4

fruity

fresh

tangy

50 g (2 oz) **butter**

2 tablespoons **golden syrup**

150 g (5 oz) **digestive biscuits**, finely crushed

Filling:

250 g (8 oz) **mascarpone cheese**

200 g (7 oz) **fromage frais**

50 g (2 oz) **caster sugar**

grated rind and juice of 2 **limes**

150 ml (¼ pint) **double cream**

To decorate:

250 g (8 oz) **strawberries**, sliced

125 g (4 oz) **blueberries**

450 g (15½ oz) pack ready-rolled **shortcrust pastry**, thawed if frozen

Filling:

25 g (1 oz) **cornflour**

100 g (3½ oz) **caster sugar**

150 ml (¼ pint) **water**

finely grated rind of 2 **lemons**

juice of 1 **lemon**

25 g (1 oz) **butter**

2 **egg yolks**

Meringue:

3 **egg whites**

175 g (6 oz) **caster sugar**

PREP

20

COOK

45

SERVES

6

gooey

mates

posh

lemon meringue pie

The combination of the crunchy pastry, soft and gooey lemon filling and marshmallowy meringue is absolutely sublime. Served hot or cold, this really will melt in your mouth!

1 Heat the oven to 220°C (425°F), Gas Mark 7.

2 Lay the pastry over the inside of a greased 23 cm (9 inch) tin. Push into place and prick the base with a fork. Cover with greaseproof paper and fill with a layer of dried beans. Bake for 10 minutes. Remove the paper and beans and bake for another 10–12 minutes until crisp. Remove from the oven and turn the temperature down to 200°C (400°F), Gas Mark 6.

3 Make the filling. Mix the cornflour and sugar in a saucepan with the water, lemon rind and juice. Bring to the boil, stirring well, until the sauce is thick and smooth. Take off the heat and stir in the butter then leave to cool slightly.

4 Whisk the egg yolks with 2 tablespoons of the sauce, then return this mixture to the pan. Cook until the sauce has thickened and pour it into the pastry case. Return to the oven for 15 minutes until the filling has set.

5 Beat the egg whites until they stand in stiff peaks. Whisk in 1 tablespoon of sugar, then fold in the rest. Spread the mixture over the filling and bake in the oven for 10 minutes.

citrus crush

125 g (4 oz) **caster sugar**

150 ml (¼ pint) **water**

1 **pink** or **ruby grapefruit**, scrubbed and halved

2 **oranges**, scrubbed and halved

1 **lime**, scrubbed and halved

Light and refreshing, this palate-cleansing pudding is perfect if you're suffering after a heavy night out.

1 Put the sugar and water into a saucepan. Bring to the boil and cook until the sugar dissolves. Remove from the heat and leave to cool.

2 Squeeze the juice from the fruit. Scoop out the membranes from the fruit shells with a spoon and keep the shells for serving. Sieve the fruit juices into the sugar syrup, then pour into a shallow plastic container to a depth of no more than 2.5 cm (1 inch).

3 Freeze the citrus mixture for 2 hours, until mushy, then beat it with a fork to break up the ice crystals. Return the mixture to the freezer for a further 2 hours, beating every 30 minutes, until the mixture looks like finely crushed ice.

4 Scoop the iced dessert into the fruit shells and serve.

fresh

cool

fab!

* + freezing

125 g (4 oz) **plain dark chocolate**, finely chopped

3 tablespoons **water**

4 **eggs**, separated

125 g (4 oz) **caster sugar**

300 ml (½ pint) **double cream**

To top:

8 tablespoons **double cream**, whipped

grated **chocolate**

PREP

20*

COOK

0

SERVES

8

best

sexy

feast

iced chocolate mousse

Can there be anyone who won't drool at the thought of these luscious little chocolate puddings? Pure heaven!

1 Put the chocolate and the water in a heatproof bowl and heat over a saucepan of simmering water until melted. Take off the heat and leave to cool slightly.

2 Whisk the egg yolks and sugar in a bowl until thick and fluffy.

3 Whisk the chocolate into the egg yolk mixture. Whip the cream until it stands in soft peaks, then fold into the chocolate mixture.

4 Whisk the egg whites until stiff. Fold 1 tablespoon into the mousse, then fold in the rest. Pour the mousse into 8 small dishes (or 1 large one) and chill in the fridge. Decorate with whipped cream and grated chocolate.

* + chilling

quick tiramisu

15*

COOK

0

SERVES

4

This unbelievably rich Italian classic is a real delight and will certainly impress your mates. In fact, if you serve this you might find it hard to get rid of them!

1 In a bowl mix together the coffee with 2 tablespoons of the sugar and the liqueur. Toss the sponge fingers in the mixture then pour them into a glass dish.

2 Beat together the custard, mascarpone and vanilla and spoon a third of the mixture over the biscuits. Sprinkle with the rest of the sugar, then add half the remaining custard. Scatter the chopped chocolate over the top, then spread with the rest of the custard.

3 Chill for about 1 hour in the fridge until set. A true delight.

* + chilling

boozy

fancy

yum!

5 tablespoons strong **espresso coffee**

75 g (3 oz) **soft brown sugar**

4 tablespoons **coffee liqueur** or 3 tablespoons **brandy**

75 g (3 oz) **sponge finger biscuits**, broken into large pieces

400 g (13 oz) ready-made **custard**

250 g (8 oz) **mascarpone cheese**

1 teaspoon **vanilla essence**

50 g (2 oz) **plain dark chocolate**, finely chopped

300 g (10 oz) **plain flour**

250 g (8 oz) **butter**, cut into cubes

25 g (1 oz) **sugar**

4–6 tablespoons cold **water**

Filling:

100 g (3½ oz) **brown sugar**

4 tablespoons **dark treacle** or **molasses**

4 tablespoons **golden syrup**

6 tablespoons **butter**, melted

1 teaspoon **vanilla essence**

grated rind of 1 **lemon**

4 **eggs**, beaten

175 g (6 oz) **pecan nuts**

PREP

25*

COOK

50

SERVES

8

snack

pals

crisp

pecan pie

A classic American dish, the rich sweetness of the filling and the crunchiness of the pecan nuts combine superbly. Just dollop on the ice cream or cream and dream away.

1 To make the pastry, put the flour in a bowl, add the butter and rub it in with your fingertips until it looks like breadcrumbs. Stir in the sugar, then add enough water to make a firm dough. Knead the pastry on a lightly floured surface, then roll out and line a 28 × 18 cm (11 × 7 inch) shallow Swiss roll tin or similar. Chill for 30 minutes.

2 Heat the oven to 180°C (350°F), Gas Mark 4.

3 To make the filling, mix the sugar, treacle, syrup, butter and vanilla essence in a bowl. Stir in the lemon rind and eggs and mix well. Chop half the pecans and add to the filling, then pour into the pie crust.

4 Dot the rest of the pecans over the top of the pie. Bake in the oven for 45–50 minutes, until the pie is golden brown and the filling has set. Leave to cool, then cut into squares and dish up.

* + chilling

warm espresso chocolate pots

It may cost a bit more, but make sure you use good quality dark chocolate with a high percentage of cocoa butter – at least 75 per cent. You will really notice the difference.

1 Put the chocolate in a saucepan with the coffee and whisky and heat very gently until the chocolate has melted. Add the sugar and stir until dissolved. Take off the heat.

2 Immediately beat in the egg yolks until the mixture thickens. Pour through a sieve into 8 espresso cups or small dishes. Cool and chill in the fridge for 4 hours or longer.

3 Whip the cream and spoon a little on to each chocolate pot, then sprinkle with nutmeg. Pour a small amount of boiling water into a roasting tin to a depth of about 1 cm (½ inch). Sit the chocolate pots in the boiling water for 1 minute to warm, then remove and dish up immediately.

* + chilling

PREP

5*

COOK

5

SERVES

8

star

tasty

sweet

175 g (6 oz) **dark plain chocolate**, chopped

250 ml (8 fl oz) strong **espresso coffee**

2 tablespoons **whisky** (optional)

50 g (2 oz) **sugar**

6 **egg yolks**

50 ml (2 fl oz) **double cream**

grated **nutmeg**

100 g (3½ oz) bar **Toblerone chocolate**

50 g (2 oz) **dark plain chocolate**

2 tablespoons **double cream**

1 tablespoon **rum**

To dip:

selection of fruit including **strawberries**, **raspberries**, **cherries** and sliced **banana**

cookies

gooey

great

mates

warm nutty chocolate fondue

Juicy fruit and a wonderfully gooey and alcoholic chocolate mixture – what more could you possibly want from life?

1 Melt the two kinds of chocolate in a heatproof bowl over a saucepan of gently simmering water.

2 Pour the chocolate into the fondue pot and add the cream. Stir well then add the rum and continue to heat, stirring, for 1 minute.

3 Move the fondue pot to the table and keep warm on a burner. Dip a selection of fruits and cookies into the chocolate and enjoy!

raspberry mallow fondue

Treating yourself to something sweet is great therapy – nothing is more likely to cheer you up or make you feel decidedly naughty!

1 Put the raspberries into a blender or food processor and blend until smooth.

2 Put the raspberries, marshmallows and cream in the fondue pot and melt over a low heat, stirring constantly. Add the lemon juice and heat, but do not allow to boil.

3 Move the fondue pot to the table and keep warm on a burner, then gather all your friends round and dip the cookies into the raspberry mallow.

PREP

5

COOK

10

SERVES

4

sweet

saucy

party

250 g (8 oz) **raspberries**

175 g (6 oz) **marshmallows**

175 ml (6 fl oz) **double cream**

few drops of **lemon juice**

To dip:

cookies

brilliant
baking

scones

250 g (8 oz) **plain flour**

½ teaspoon **salt**

4 teaspoons **baking powder**

50 g (2 oz) **butter**, softened and cut into cubes

150 ml (¼ pint) **milk**

a little **water**

milk or **flour**, to finish

PREP

12

COOK

10

SERVES

12

snack

best

hot

These scones are very quick and easy to make. Best scoffed warm from the oven with dollops of clotted cream and jam.

1 Heat the oven to 230°C (450°F), Gas Mark 8.

2 Mix the flour, salt and baking powder in a large bowl. Add the butter and rub in with your fingertips until it looks like breadcrumbs. Make a hole in the centre, pour in the milk and mix to a soft spongy dough, adding a little water if it needs it.

3 Knead the dough lightly on a well-floured surface. Roll out or flatten until it is 1.5 cm (¾ inch) thick. Cut into 6 cm (2½ inch) circles, using a glass as a guide. Put on a baking sheet.

4 Gather the extra dough into a ball then flatten and cut out more circles. Brush the scones with milk for a glazed finish or rub with flour for a soft crust. Bake in the oven for 7–10 minutes until well risen and golden on top.

5 Split open the scones and spread with butter, cream and jam.

vanilla fairy cakes

These cakes are easy and fun to make. When you've perfected this recipe why not try out some of the variations given below?

1 Heat the oven to 180°C (350°F), Gas Mark 4.

2 Put all the ingredients in a large bowl and beat until light and creamy. Divide the mixture evenly among 12 paper cake cases.

3 Bake in the oven for 18–20 minutes until risen and just firm to the touch then put on a wire rack or plate to cool.

Variations:

Chocolate: Add 15 g (½ oz) cocoa powder instead of 15 g (½ oz) of the flour.

Chocolate chip: Add 50 g (2 oz) plain dark, milk or white chocolate chips.

Coffee: Add 1 tablespoon espresso or strong coffee powder.

Citrus: Add the finely grated rind of 1 lemon or 1 small orange.

Cranberry or blueberry: Add 75 g (3 oz) dried cranberries or blueberries, chopped if large.

PREP

10

COOK

20

MAKES

12

great

easy

fun

150 g (5 oz) **butter** or **margarine**, softened

150 g (5 oz) **caster sugar**

175 g (6 oz) **self-raising flour**

3 **eggs**

1 teaspoon **vanilla essence**

125 g (4 oz) **butter** or **margarine**, plus extra for greasing

125 g (4 oz) **caster sugar**

2 **eggs**

125 g (4 oz) **self-raising flour**

1 tablespoon hot **water**

To fill and top:

150 ml (¼ pint) **double cream**, lightly whipped

3 tablespoons **jam**

icing sugar

15

COOK

25

SERVES

8

super

party

tasty

victoria sandwich cake

Turn this light sponge cake into a real treat by sandwiching the layers with whipped cream as well as jam.

1 Heat the oven to 180°C (350°F), Gas Mark 4. Line and grease two 18 cm (7 inch) cake tins.

2 Mix together the butter and sugar until light and fluffy. Beat in the eggs, one at a time, adding a tablespoon of the flour with the second egg. Fold in the rest of the flour, then the water.

3 Divide the mixture between the two tins and bake in the oven for 20–25 minutes, until the cakes are golden and springy. Turn out on to a wire rack or plate and leave to cool.

4 Sandwich the cakes together with the cream and jam and sprinkle the top with icing sugar. Perfect!

chocolate cake

PREP

15

COOK

50

SERVES

8

This is so easy to make that you have to try it. The deliciously rich texture makes it good for a pudding, too – just serve with whipped cream or vanilla ice cream.

1 Heat the oven to 160°C (325°F), Gas Mark 3. Line and grease a 23 cm (9 inch) cake tin.

2 Mix all the dry ingredients together in a large bowl and make a hole in the centre. Add the golden syrup, eggs, oil and milk and beat thoroughly until smooth.

3 Pour into the cake tin and bake in the oven for 45–50 minutes. Leave in the tin for a few minutes then turn out on to a wire rack or plate to cool.

4 To make the icing, put the chocolate and cream into a small saucepan and heat gently, stirring, until melted. Leave to cool slightly, then pour over the cake. Beautiful!

gooey

feast

sexy

200 g (7 oz) **plain flour**

1 teaspoon **bicarbonate of soda**

1 teaspoon **baking powder**

2 tablespoons **cocoa powder**

150 g (5 oz) **soft brown sugar**

2 tablespoons **golden syrup**

2 **eggs**

150 ml (¼ pint) **vegetable oil**

150 ml (¼ pint) **milk**

Chocolate icing

175 g (6 oz) **plain dark chocolate**

2 tablespoons **single cream**

250 g (8 oz) **self-raising flour**

½ teaspoon ground **mixed spice**

½ teaspoon ground **cinnamon**

125 g (4 oz) **butter** or **margarine**

125 g (4 oz) **soft brown sugar**

125 g (4 oz) **currants**

50 g (2 oz) **glacé cherries**, quartered

1 large **egg**

5 tablespoons **milk**

PREP

COOK

SERVES

tangy

fast

mates

really easy fruit cake

As the name suggests, all you really have to do is mix all the ingredients together and chuck them in the oven. Then all you need is a cup is a tea …

1 Heat the oven to 180°C (350°F), Gas Mark 4. Line and grease a 20 cm (8 inch) square cake tin.

2 Mix the flour, mixed spice and cinnamon in a large bowl, add the butter and rub in with your fingertips until the mixture looks like breadcrumbs. Stir in the sugar, currants and glacé cherries.

3 Whisk the egg and milk together, add to the fruit mixture and beat thoroughly.

4 Pour the mixture into the cake tin and bake in the oven for 1¼–1½ hours. Leave for a few minutes then turn out on to a wire rack or plate to cool.

chocolate and banana teabread

Chocolate and banana work together really well, and by layering the chocolate you get a beautiful rippled effect.

1 Heat the oven to 180°C (350°F), Gas Mark 4. Grease a 1 kg (2 lb) loaf tin.

2 Put the chocolate in a heatproof bowl with the ginger and 25 g (1 oz) of the butter. Place over a saucepan of simmering water until melted.

3 Meanwhile, mash the bananas.

4 Put the rest of the butter into a bowl with the sugar and beat until creamy. Add the eggs, banana, flour and baking powder and beat together until smooth.

5 Spread a quarter of the creamed mixture into the tin, then spoon over a third of the chocolate mixture. Spread with another quarter of the cake mixture, then more chocolate. Repeat the layering, finishing with a layer of the cake mixture.

6 Scatter the chopped chocolate down the centre of the cake. Bake in the oven for about 1 hour until a sharp knife inserted into the centre comes out clean. Leave in the tin for 10 minutes then tip out on to a wire rack to cool completely.

PREP

20

COOK

60

SERVES

10

star

pals

moist

200 g (7 oz) **plain dark chocolate**, broken into pieces

½ teaspoon ground **ginger**

200 g (7 oz) **butter** or **margarine**, softened

2 ripe **bananas**

175 g (6 oz) **caster sugar**

3 **eggs**

250 g (8 oz) **self-raising flour**

⅛ teaspoon **baking powder**

50 g (2 oz) **plain dark chocolate**, chopped

swiss roll

3 **eggs**

75 g (3 oz) **caster sugar**

75 g (3 oz) **plain flour**

1 tablespoon hot **water**

caster sugar

3 tablespoons
strawberry jam

Use whatever kind of jam you like in this roll – you can also add whipped cream or butter icing if you really want to tart it up.

1 Heat the oven to 200°C (400°F), Gas Mark 6. Line and grease an 18 × 28 cm (7 × 11 inch) Swiss roll tin or similar.

2 Whisk the eggs and sugar in a large bowl over a saucepan of hot water until thick and creamy. Fold in the flour and the water, then pour into the Swiss roll tin.

3 Bake in the oven for 8–10 minutes, until the cake is springy.

4 Sprinkle sugar on to greaseproof paper, then tip the cake on to it. Peel off the lining paper and trim off the edges of the cake so they are neat, then spread with the jam and roll up. Hold in position for a few minutes, then put on a wire rack or plate to cool. Sprinkle more caster sugar over the top, then slice and eat.

triple chocolate muffins

These are best eaten on the day they are made, but they are unlikely to last longer than a few minutes anyway as they smell and taste so good.

1 Heat the oven to 200°C (400°F), Gas Mark 6.

2 Put 175 g (6 oz) of the chocolate in a heatproof bowl and melt over a saucepan of simmering water. Stir in the melted butter and take off the heat.

3 Beat together the egg and milk and slowly beat this mixture into the melted chocolate.

4 Mix the flour, baking powder, cocoa powder and sugar in a bowl. Add the chocolate mixture with the rest of the plain chocolate and the chocolate buttons to the dry ingredients and fold together until just combined.

5 Divide the mixture among 12 paper muffin cases. Bake in the oven for 20–25 minutes until well risen and just firm. Delicious warm or cold.

mates

posh

gooey

300 g (10 oz) **plain dark chocolate**, chopped

50 g (2 oz) **butter**, melted

1 **egg**

350 ml (12 fl oz) **milk**

375 g (12 oz) **self-raising flour**

1 tablespoon **baking powder**

50 g (2 oz) **cocoa powder**

100 g (3½ oz) **caster sugar**

75 g (3 oz) **white chocolate buttons**

125 g (4 oz) **butter** or **margarine**

2 tablespoons **golden syrup**

25 g (1 oz) **cocoa powder**

250 g (8 oz) **puffed rice**

125 g (4 oz) **dried cranberries** or **raisins**

PREP

COOK

MAKES

telly

sweet

quick

chocolate crunch crisps

If you prefer, use 50 g (2 oz) of desiccated coconut instead of the cocoa powder, or try using corn flakes instead of the puffed rice.

1 Put the butter and golden syrup in a large saucepan and heat, stirring, until melted.

2 Add the cocoa powder and mix well, then add the puffed rice and cranberries and stir until evenly coated.

3 Divide the mixture among 20 paper sweet cases and chill until set.

spice biscuits

PREP

15

COOK

20

MAKES

15

A great snack, these tasty biscuits will fill your kitchen with the most wonderful smell of baking.

1 Heat the oven to 180°C (350°F), Gas Mark 4.

2 In a bowl beat the butter and sugar until smooth and fluffy, then beat in the potato.

3 Add the flour, sultanas and mixed spice and mix well. Roll out on a lightly floured surface to 5 mm (¼ inch) thick. Cut out 6 cm (2½ inch) circles, using a glass as a guide, and put them on greased baking sheets.

4 Bake in the oven for 15–20 minutes until golden brown. Leave to cool, then tuck in.

tasty

spicy

keeps

125 g (4 oz) **butter** or **margarine**, plus extra for greasing

50 g (2 oz) **soft brown sugar**

50 g (2 oz) cold mashed **potato**

175 g (6 oz) **brown rice flour**

50 g (2 oz) **sultanas**

1 teaspoon **mixed spice**

125 g (4 oz) **butter**, softened, plus extra for greasing

150 g (5 oz) **caster sugar**

1 **egg**, beaten

1 teaspoon **baking powder**

125 g (4 oz) crunchy **peanut butter**

150 g (5 oz) **plain flour**

100 g (3½ oz) **dried banana chunks**, roughly chopped

28 unsalted **peanuts**

PREP

COOK

MAKES

28

crisp

cheap

light

peanut butter and banana cookies

Don't be put off by what seems like a slightly strange combination – these cookies are irresistibly tempting.

1 Heat the oven to 190°C (375°F), Gas Mark 5. Grease two large baking sheets.

2 Put all the ingredients, except the banana chunks and peanuts, in a blender or food processor and blend until well mixed. Stir in the banana chunks.

3 On a lightly floured surface roll the dough into balls about the size of a walnut and place them on the baking sheets, allowing enough space for the mixture to spread as it cooks. Using the palm of your hand, flatten the balls slightly.

4 Press a whole peanut into the centre of each cookie and bake in the oven for 10–15 minutes, or until starting to brown around the edges.

5 Leave to cool slightly then move on to a wire rack or plate and leave to cool completely.

chunky oat cookies

Use good-quality white chocolate because cheap chocolate has a rather cloying taste. If you prefer, use milk or plain dark chocolate.

1 Heat the oven to 180°C (350°F), Gas Mark 4. Grease a large baking sheet.

2 Beat together the butter and sugar in a bowl until creamy. Add the egg, vanilla, oats, sunflower seeds, flour and baking powder and mix to make a thick paste. Stir in the chocolate.

3 Place dessertspoonfuls of the mixture on to the baking sheet and flatten slightly with the back of a fork.

4 Bake in the oven for about 15 minutes until risen and golden. Leave for 5 minutes, then move to a wire rack or plate to cool.

PREP

10

COOK

15

MAKES

15

pals

fab!

great

125 g (4 oz) **butter**, softened, plus extra for greasing

125 g (4 oz) **caster sugar**

1 **egg**

2 teaspoons **vanilla essence**

125 g (4 oz) **porridge oats**

4 tablespoons **sunflower seeds**

150 g (5 oz) **plain flour**

½ teaspoon **baking powder**

175 g (6 oz) **white chocolate**, chopped into small pieces

125 g (4 oz) **butter** or **margarine**, plus extra for greasing

50 g (2 oz) **brown sugar**

2 tablespoons **golden syrup**

250 g (8 oz) **rolled oats**

1 tablespoon **dried cranberries**

PREP

COOK

MAKES

fills

crisp

fruity

cranberry flapjacks

These crunchy biscuits are always popular, and this variation, which adds delicious cranberries, tastes even better than more traditional recipes.

1 Heat the oven to 180°C (350°F), Gas Mark 4. Grease a 20 cm (8 inch) square sandwich tin or similar.

2 Put the butter, sugar and syrup into a saucepan and heat gently until melted. Take the pan off the heat and add the oats and cranberries, mixing thoroughly.

3 Spoon the mixture into the tin and smooth it out. Bake in the oven for about 30 minutes or until golden brown.

4 Leave the flapjacks to cool in the tin for about 5 minutes then mark into 16 portions. Leave to cool completely so they go crunchy, then remove from the tin. Extremely moreish!

crumble jam squares

This tempting tea-time treat also makes a great pudding when served with custard.

1 Heat the oven to 200°C (400°F), Gas Mark 6. Grease a 32 × 23 cm (13 × 9 inch) cake tin or similar.

2 Put all the ingredients except the jam in a large bowl and beat the mixture until it is crumbly. Put 3–4 tablespoons of the mixture to one side, then press the rest into the tin. Spread evenly with the jam then sprinkle over the rest of the mixture.

3 Bake in the oven for 30 minutes until golden. Leave to cool in the tin then cut into squares.

PREP

10

COOK

30

MAKES

24

super

feast

party

175 g (6 oz) **rolled oats**

175 g (6 oz) **plain rice flour**

250 g (8 oz) **butter** or **margarine**, plus extra for greasing

125 g (4 oz) **soft brown sugar**

50 g (2 oz) mixed **dried fruit**, chopped

1 teaspoon **cinnamon**

½ teaspoon **bicarbonate of soda**

5 tablespoons **cherry jam**

cocktails

classic pimm's

3

1

party

1 measure **Pimm's No 1**

3–4 **ice cubes**

2–3 slices of **orange**, **lemon**, and **cucumber**

3 measures **lemonade**

The drink of the summer ... all you need is the sunshine to go with it!

1 Pour the Pimm's into a tall glass and add the ice cubes.

2 Add the fruit and cucumber slices, then add the lemonade. Delicious!

mint julep

3

1

sexy

3 **mint** sprigs

½ teaspoon **caster sugar**

1 tablespoon **soda water**

2–3 **ice cubes**, crushed

1 measure **Bourbon whiskey**

mint sprig

The official drink of the Kentucky Derby, this is a true thirst-quencher.

1 Crush the mint with the caster sugar in a small bowl then rub it around the inside of a tall glass. Chuck out the mint.

2 Pour in the soda water, add the ice then pour over the Bourbon. Do not stir. Top with the mint.

kir

2 **ice cubes**

1 measure **crème de cassis**

4 measures **dry white wine**

This popular French aperitif is made from blackcurrant-flavoured liqueur and white wine. For a Kir Royale, use champagne instead of wine.

1 Put the ice cubes into a wine glass.

2 Pour the crème de cassis and wine over the ice, stir gently and serve.

bellini

2 measures **peach juice**

4 measures chilled **champagne**

1 dash of **grenadine**

slice of **peach**

raspberries

This bubbly and elegant drink is irresistible and will slip down far too easily ... watch out for that hangover!

1 Mix all the ingredients in a large wine glass.

2 Serve decorated with a peach slice and raspberries on a cocktail stick.

fruity

moscow mule

3–4 **ice cubes**, cracked

2 measures **vodka**

juice of 2 **limes**

ginger beer, to top

slice of **lime**

A classic cocktail choice, this will certainly put you in the mood for a good night out. If you swap the vodka for tequila you'll have a Mexican Mule instead …

1 Put the cracked ice into a cocktail shaker or screw-top jar. Add the vodka and lime juice and shake until a frost forms.

2 Pour into a large tumbler and top with ginger beer. Decorate with a slice of lime and drink through a straw.

bloody mary

ice cubes

juice of ½ **lemon**

2 dashes of vegetarian **Worcestershire sauce**

2 dashes of **Tabasco sauce**

100 ml (4 fl oz) thick **tomato juice**

2 measures **vodka**

salt and **pepper**

celery stick

Attributed to Harry's Bar in Paris, this spicy mix of vodka and tomato juice not only makes a great drink but is a good hangover cure the next day.

1 Put some ice cubes into a cocktail shaker or screw-top jar. Add the lemon juice, Worcestershire sauce, Tabasco sauce, tomato juice and vodka.

2 Shake well, then strain into a tall glass over 4–6 ice cubes, add a pinch of salt and a pinch of pepper and stick in a celery stick.

black russian

A true classic, this sweet, strong and smooth cocktail is a knockout!

1 Put some cracked ice into a short glass.

2 Add the vodka and Kahlúa and stir well. Decorate with a chocolate stick.

PREP

2

SERVES

1

fab!

3 **ice cubes**, cracked

2 measures **vodka**

1 measure **Kahlúa**

chocolate stick

white russian

A creamy version of the Black Russian. If you don't have Kahlúa you can use Tia Maria.

1 Put half the ice cubes into a cocktail shaker or screw-top jar and add the vodka, Kahlúa and double cream. Shake well.

2 Put the rest of the ice cubes into a tall glass and strain in the cocktail. Drink through a straw.

PREP

3

SERVES

1

super

5 **ice cubes**, cracked

1 measure **vodka**

1 measure **Kahlúa**

1 measure **double cream**

5–6 **ice cubes**

½ measure **dry vermouth**

3 measures **gin**

1 **green olive**

dry martini

Reputedly named after its creator, a New York barman called Martini, you can have this either shaken or stirred …

1 Put the ice cubes into a large glass. Pour the vermouth and gin over the ice and stir or shake.

2 Strain into a chilled cocktail glass. Serve with a green olive on a cocktail stick.

4–5 **ice cubes**

juice of ½ **lemon**

1 measure **cherry brandy**

3 measures **gin**

soda water

PREP

SERVES

gin sling

For the full effect, decorate with cherries and drink with a straw.

1 Put the ice cubes into a cocktail shaker or screw-top jar. Add the lemon juice, cherry brandy and gin and shake until a frost forms.

2 Pour into a glass and top up with soda water.

between the sheets

Very tasty but rather strong – you will need to pace yourself with this one.

1   Put the ice cubes into a cocktail shaker or screw-top jar. Add the brandy, white rum, Cointreau, lemon juice and sugar syrup and shake until a frost forms.

2   Pour into a chilled cocktail glass and sip.

PREP

SERVES

fun

4–5 **ice cubes**

1¼ measures **brandy**

1 measure **white rum**

½ measure **Cointreau**

¾ measure **lemon juice**

½ measure **sugar syrup** (½ sugar and ½ boiling water)

tijuana sling

A long drink with a very intriguing mix of flavours – tequila, blackcurrant, lime and ginger. Definitely one to try!

1   Pour the tequila, crème de cassis, lime juice and bitters into a cocktail shaker or screw-top jar.

2   Add some ice cubes and shake vigorously. Pour into a glass then top up with ginger ale.

PREP

SERVES

tasty

1¼ measures **tequila**

¾ measure **crème de cassis**

juice of 2 **limes**

2 dashes **Peychaud's bitters**

4–5 **ice cubes**

ginger ale, to top

cuba libre

2–3 **ice cubes**

1½ measures **dark rum**

juice of ½ **lime**

cola, to top up

slice of **lime**

Although Cuba has always been known for its light – rather than dark – rum, dark rum is the main ingredient in this strong cocktail.

1 Put the ice cubes in a tall glass and pour the rum and lime juice over them.

2 Stir well then top up with cola, decorate with a slice of lime and drink with a straw.

mojito

12 **mint leaves** or small sprigs

½ measure **sugar syrup** (½ sugar and ½ boiling water)

1 **lime**, cut into 6 wedges

3–4 **ice cubes**, crushed

2 measures **white rum**

soda water

A real crowd pleaser, this classic Cuban cocktail is made with refreshing mint leaves. Perfect for those long summer evenings.

1 Mix the mint, sugar syrup and 4 of the lime wedges in a glass.

2 Fill the glass with crushed ice, add the rum and stir, then top up with soda water. Decorate with the rest of the lime wedges.

irish coffee

The perfect after-dinner drink, this delightful blend of strong coffee, Irish whiskey and a little sugar is topped by a float of double cream.

SERVES

1

1 Place a spoon in a large wine glass, add the whiskey, then top up with coffee and stir.

2 Heat the cream very slightly and pour over the back of the spoon on top of the coffee to get a good float. Decorate with a pinch of ground coffee.

boozy

25 ml (1 fl oz) **Irish whiskey**

hot **filter coffee**

lightly whipped **double cream**

sprinkle of **ground coffee**

egg nog

PREP

5

A traditional drink, a glass of egg nog will quickly warm you up to the bottom of your stomach.

SERVES

1

1 Put the brandy, rum, egg and sugar syrup into a cocktail shaker or screw-top jar and shake well, then strain into a large goblet.

2 Add the milk, sprinkle with grated nutmeg and sip.

hot!

1 measure **brandy**

1 measure **dark rum**

1 **egg**

1 teaspoon **sugar syrup** (½ teaspoon sugar and ½ teaspoon boiling water)

75 ml (3 fl oz) **milk**

grated **nutmeg**, to top

pinch of **salt**

1 measure **gold tequila**

slice of **lemon**

party

tequila shot

Traditionally tequila shots have to be drunk in one – just prepare yourself for the kick immediately afterwards!

1 Lick the salt, drink the shot, bite the lemon!

---

1 measure **gold tequila**

1 measure **champagne**

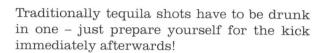

pals

tequila slammer

Tequila is often drunk as a slammer, and this is the original but glamorous version.

1 Pour the tequila into a shot glass and slowly top up with champagne. Cover the top of the glass with the palm of your hand and grip it tightly.

2 Briskly pick up the glass and slam it down on a surface to make the drink fizz. Quickly gulp it down in one, while it's still fizzing.

kamikaze shooter

A classic shot featuring vodka, Cointreau and lime juice. The only way to drink it is to down it in one.

1 Put the vodka, Cointreau and lime juice into a cocktail shaker or screw-top jar with some ice cubes.

2 Shake briefly, then strain into a shot glass.

PREP

SERVES

¾ measure **vodka**

¾ measure **Cointreau**

½ measure fresh **lime juice**

ice cubes

cowgirl

The flavour of peach schnapps with Bailey's is a winning combination, and the slice of ripe peach adds a touch of decadence to this shot.

1 Pour the schnapps into a shot glass, then carefully pour a layer of Bailey's on top.

2 Place a peach wedge on the rim of the glass, down the shot, then eat the wedge.

PREP

SERVES

1 measure chilled **peach schnapps**

½ measure **Bailey's Irish Cream**

peach wedge

beat the hangover

Note
You'll need a proper juicer for these recipes, but it's a good investment. There are several different types so it's worth shopping around.

100 g (3½ oz) **tomatoes**

200 g (7 oz) **cabbage**

large handful of **parsley**

celery stick

raw energy

Not only will this juice boost your energy levels and help you lose that sluggish feeling, but it has the added – and necessary – benefit of freshening your breath!

1 Juice the tomatoes, cabbage and parsley, pour into a glass and chuck in a stick of celery to nibble on. Very refreshing.

½ **grapefruit**, peeled

100 g (3½ oz) **celery**

100 g (3½ oz) **fennel**

ice cubes, crushed

PREP

SERVES

mother nature

If you can't lift your head off the pillow because it is throbbing so badly, you will find this juice brilliantly restorative. You might need to persuade a friend to make it for you!

1 Juice the grapefruit, celery and fennel, then pour into a glass over the ice and drink immediately.

hangover express

This is a super juice, especially if you've had a few too many cocktails the night before. Broccoli is a great antioxidant and stimulates the liver while apples are superb detoxifiers.

1 Juice the broccoli, apples and spinach, alternating the spinach with the broccoli and apple so that the machine doesn't get clogged up with the leaves. This juice is very sweet, so mix with a couple of ice cubes before serving.

PREP

SERVES

fast

150 g (5 oz) **broccoli**

2 **apples**

150 g (5 oz) **spinach**

ice cubes

live wire

This rich and sweet juice is really good for your liver, which is very important if you have over-indulged the night before.

1 Juice the grapes, beetroot and plums then pour into a glass with the ice cubes.

PREP

SERVES

juicy

100 g (3½ oz) **red grapes**

100 g (3½ oz) **beetroot**

100 g (3½ oz) **plums**

ice cubes

100 g (3½ oz) **lettuce**

½ **lemon**, peeled

100 ml (3½ fl oz) chilled **camomile tea**

ice cubes

crisp

mind bath

Lettuce is ideal for calming a throbbing head, If your liver is feeling the strain, substitute the calming effects of camomile tea for the detoxifying powers of dandelion leaf tea.

1 Juice the lettuce and lemon then mix with the chilled camomile tea. Serve over ice.

100 g (3½ oz) **celeriac**

100 g (3½ oz) **Jerusalem artichokes**

100 g (3½ oz) **celery**

small bunch of **mint**

ice cubes

fab!

gargle blaster

As well as freshening your breath, mint is a great source of potassium. The celery also helps your body to detox more efficiently. A very healthy pick-me-up.

1 Peel the celeriac and chop it into sticks. Scrub the artichokes. Juice the vegetables and the mint, alternating the mint leaves with the other ingredients to prevent the juicer from getting clogged up.

2 Pour into a glass over the ice cubes and drink straight away.

upbeet

PREP

You may find the juice a little bitter, so if you don't like the taste just remind yourself it's a very effective hangover cure.

1 Juice all the ingredients, then pour over the ice and drink straight away.

SERVES

cool

100 g (3½ oz) **celeriac**, peeled

50 g (2 oz) **beetroot**

100 g (3½ oz) **carrots**

50 g (2 oz) **radicchio**

1 **apple**

ice cubes, crushed

st clements

PREP

5

Orange juice is a well-known hangover cure as it's high in vitamin C and potassium, plus it tastes deliciously fresh and zingy. Just what you need first thing in the morning ...

1 Peel the oranges and lemon then juice. Put the ice in a tumbler, pour over the juice and glug down.

SERVES

1

yum!

3 **oranges**

½ **lemon**

4 **ice cubes**, crushed

banana shake

PREP

SERVES

1 **banana**, chopped

juice of 1 **orange**

1 teaspoon **clear honey**

300 ml (½ pint) **milk**

8 **ice cubes**

pinch of ground
cinnamon

This is really good for sorting you out when you are suffering from a late night. The honey will give you an instant energy boost, while the banana will give you longer lasting energy.

1 Put the banana, orange juice, honey and milk in a blender or food processor and blend until smooth.

2 Tip the ice into two glasses, pour in the drink and sprinkle with cinnamon.

bugs bunny

PREP

SERVES

4–6 **ice cubes**

50 ml (2 fl oz) **carrot juice**

50 ml (2 fl oz) **orange juice**

dash of **Tabasco sauce**

1 **celery stick**

A little kick of spice to get your brain going, combined with the rehydrating effects of the juice, makes this a fantastic drink if you need to get on with your work.

1 Put the ice cubes into a tumbler, pour in the carrot juice and orange juice then add a dash of Tabasco sauce and stir with the celery stick.

cranberry crush

If you feel as if your kidneys are suffering from working too hard, then this warm cranberry-based drink is the one for you.

1 Put the cranberry and orange juices, water, ginger and mixed spice into a saucepan and bring gently to the boil, then stir in the sugar.

2 Simmer for 5 minutes then leave to cool slightly before pouring into the glasses.

PREP

5

SERVES
2

juicy

125 ml (4 fl oz) **cranberry juice**

125 ml (4 fl oz) fresh **orange juice**

25 ml (1 fl oz) **water**

pinch of ground **ginger**

pinch of **mixed spice**

pinch of **sugar**

appleade

This is perfect if your stomach is rebelling from a battering the night before. A deliciously fresh and cool drink, the apple is packed with nutrients that will help you recover.

1 Chop the apples and put them in a large bowl. Pour the boiling water over the apples and add the sugar.

2 Leave to stand for 10 minutes, then sieve into a jug and leave to cool. Put a few ice cubes into 3 tall glasses then pour in the appleade.

PREP

5

SERVES
3

green

2 large **apples**

600 ml (1 pint) boiling **water**

½ teaspoon **sugar**

ice cubes

peach zinger

PREP

12

SERVES

4

fruity

4 **peaches**

1 tablespoon **citrus cordial**

juice of **1 lime**

crushed **ice**

300 ml (½ pint) **lemonade**

Peaches are nice and soothing, while the bubbles from the lemonade will help to ease a queasy stomach. Ideal if you and your mates are suffering from to much partying ...

1 Put the peaches in a bowl of boiling water for 1–2 minutes. Run under cold water then peel off the skins. Halve, pit and chop the flesh.

2 Put the peaches, citrus cordial and lime juice in a blender or food processor and blend until smooth.

3 Half-fill 4 tall glasses with crushed ice, add the peach and top up with lemonade.

mango and coconut lassi

PREP

10

SERVES

2

posh

1 large **mango**

juice of 1 **orange**

juice of 1 **lime**

1 tablespoon **clear honey**

300 ml (½ pint) **natural yogurt**

4 tablespoons **coconut milk**

ice cubes

A lassi is a Indian drink, so this creamy mango juice may be particularly effective if you are suffering from a late-night curry.

1 Peel the mango, cut out the stone and finely chop up the flesh.

2 Put the flesh in a blender or food processor. Add the orange juice, lime juice, honey, yogurt and coconut milk and blend until smooth. Pour into 2 glasses over the ice cubes and enjoy cold.

tropical fruit smoothie

PREP

SERVES

This satisfying smoothie provides a good source of carbohydrate to energize you for the day ahead, and pineapple is known to help with digestion.

1 Peel and slice the banana, then put it in a plastic container and freeze for at least 2 hours or overnight.

2 Peel the mango, remove the stone and roughly chop the flesh. Place in a blender or food processor with the frozen banana, yogurt and pineapple juice.

3 Blend until smooth and serve immediately.

1 large **banana**

1 large ripe **mango**

150 g (5 oz) **natural yogurt**

300 ml (½ pint) **pineapple juice**

rhubarb and custard

PREP

SERVES

Rhubarb is a great source of potassium and also contains vitamin C, which is really good for reducing the unpleasant effects of hangovers. One to get out of bed for!

1 Drain the rhubarb and put in a blender or food processor with the custard and milk.

2 Blend until smooth. Pour into a glass, add a couple of ice cubes and drink straight away.

150 g (5 oz) can **rhubarb**

150 g (5 oz) **ready-made custard**

100 ml (3½ fl oz) **milk**

ice cubes

index

acknowledgements
Executive Editor: Nicky Hill
Editor: Jessica Cowie
Executive Art Editor:
Tokiko Morishima
Book Design: Rozelle Bentheim
Designer: Miranda Harvey
Senior Production Controller:
Martin Croshaw
Introduction supplied by:
Cara Frost- Sharratt

With special thanks to
David Preston for his work
on the typography.